Vladimír Holan

YET
THERE
IS MUSIC

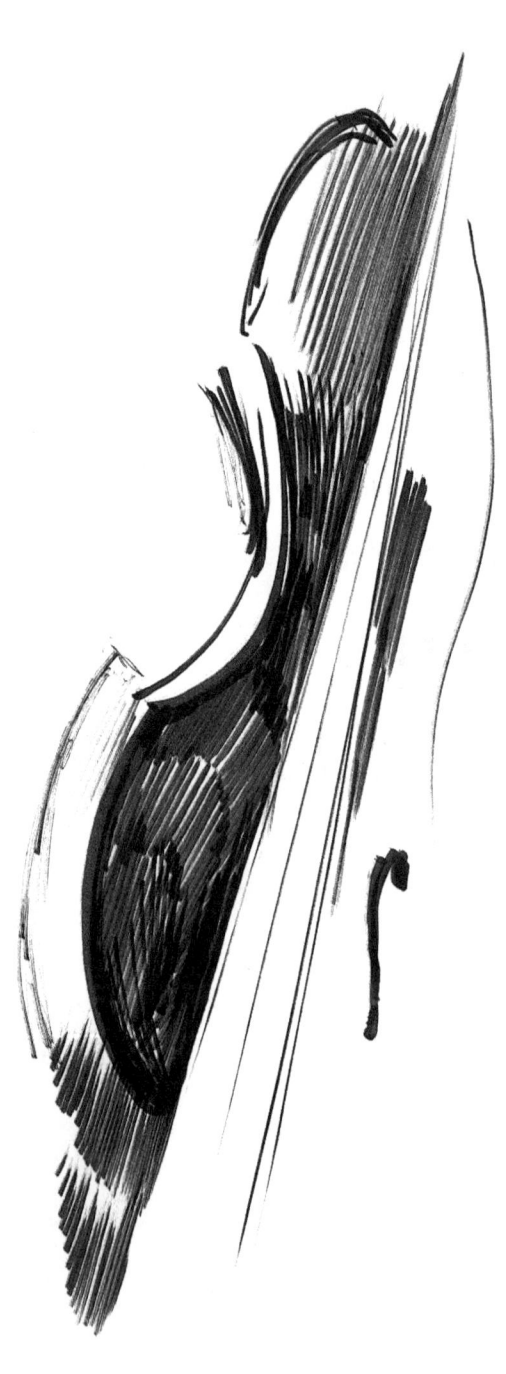

Vladimír Holan

YET
THERE
IS MUSIC

Verses from years 1939–1948

©Vladimír Holan estate, c/o Aura-pont, 2011
©Translation from Czech: Josef Tomáš, 2011
© Illustrations: Jáchym Šerých, 2011
© Introduction: Jiří Brabec, 2011

Originally published by Odeon, Praha, 1968, under the title *Ale je hudba*

All rights reserved

This book is copyright. Subject to statutory exception and to
provisions of relevant collective licensing agreements, no part of
this publication may be reproduced, stored in a retrieval system, or
transmitted in any form, or by any means, without the prior written
permission of the author's estate.

Printed and bound in the United Kingdom

Typeset in Regent and Aichel

This book is sold subject to the condition that it shall not, by way of
trade or otherwise, be lent, re-sold, hired out or otherwise circulated
without the publisher's prior consent in any form of binding or cover
other than that which it is published and without a similar condition
including this condition being imposed on the subsequent purchaser.

ISBN 978-1-84549-522-0

Published 2011 by arima publishing
ASK House, Northgate Avenue
Bury St Edmunds, Suffolk IP32 6
t: (+44)01284 700321
www.arimapublishing.com

Czech poets in arima publishing

Vladimír Holan
The First Testament, 2005
Soliloquy with Shakespeare, 2007
Narrative Poems I, 2008
Narrative Poems II, 2010
Dolour, 2011

Jiří Orten
Selected Poems, 2007

Josef Tomáš
The World in My Mouth, 2009

The translation of this book has been kindly subsidized
by the Ministry of Culture of the Czech Republic

Acknowledgement

I am indebted to Clia Goodwin, for her sensitive editing skills and helpful suggestions in the preparation of these translations.

Contents

Introduction		19
	WITHOUT A TITLE	
I	Nothing to Begin With	27
II	Discernment	28
III	Why?	29
IV	Swelter	30
V	Like no One	31
VI	A Picture that is not an Abyss	32
VII	A Triptych	33
VIII	A Funeral	34
IX	Yet	35
X	Perusing Shelley's Letters	36
XI	Ecstasy	37
XII	In the Ruins	38
XIII	Today	39
XIV	Not Only Qualms	40
XV	A Sleeping One	41
XVI	To Have	43
XVII	A Snake	44
XVIII	Out of Lovelessness	45
XIX	Deep in the Woods	46
XX	No	47
XXI	A Bitter One	48
XXII	All the Time	49
XXIII	Only in Darkness	50
XXIV	An Evening in May	51

XXV	Without a Title	52
XXVI	When?	53
XXVII	In the Groves of the Chlumec Region	54
XXVIII	A Duet	55
XXIX	By Train	56
XXX	Subidas I	57
XXXI	A Flyleaf	58
XXXII	Lovers	59
XXXIII	Subidas II	60
XXXIV	Fate	61
XXXV	At a Ferry	62
XXXVI	Real Life	63
XXXVII	As It's in the Books	64
XXXVIII	A Night in Cernohousy	65
XXXIX	The Autumn in the Mountains	66
XL	Even If	67
XLI	The Village Spring	68
XLII	A Waterfall	69
XLIII	The Bridge Across the River L.	70
XLIV	An Evening at Indian Summer	71
XLV	At a Graveyard	72
XLVI	Two Lakes	74
XLVII	Before a Storm	75
XLVIII	Verses	76
XLIX	The 31st of December	77
L	Memory of a Lunar Night near Liboc	78
LI	A Horoscope	79
LII	A Sleeping Boy	80
LIII	Rapids at the River Otava	81
LIV	A Sultry Night	82
LV	No, Don't Go Yet	83

LVI	Along a Street	84
LVII	You, Woman	85
LVIII	A Moment	86
LIX	The Noon	87
LX	I Wonder if You Recall	88
LXI	There are the Seas	89
LXII	Oh We, We Disgraced?	90
LXIII	Time Grates Its Teeth	91
LXIV	A Storm at the River	92
LXV	Somnia Et Noctium Phantasmata	93
LXVI	A Stroll	94
LXVII	A Duet II	95
LXVIII	Dialog	96
LXIX	Behind	97
LXX	But there Is Wine	98
LXXI	Suffering	99
LXXII	Eterno Nò, Ma Ben Antico	100
LXXIII	All the Time	101
LXXIV	At the Grave of K. H. Macha	102

ON THE ADVANCE

After That, Nothing	109
The Prayer of A Stone	110
Who Knows	111
Near a Footpath	112
We Know no Ends, no Bounds	113
An Evening in a Village	114
Reflection?	115
The Night Before Evening	116
Encounter I	117
Lament of One Deceased	118

While Wet	119
But Never Doubt I Love	120
You Walked By	121
Walls	122
Spring Time	123
At the End of the World	124
Encounter II	125
At a Flea Market in Paris	126
A Countryside Called Sultriness	127
At the very Source	128
En La Noche Serena	129
Deep Down	130
In a Coal Shop	131
Keats	132
Eva I	133
Coup De Grace	135
Blake	136
Crucifixion	137
Will I Be Forgiven One Day?	138
A Voice and a Counter-Voice	139
Yes, You Know –	141
A Dog Day at Chlumec	142
During the Construction of the Tower of Babel	143
Who Are You?	144
One Single Piece of History	145
Death	147
It Is Today ...	148
Life I	149
What We Have Seen on the First Day after the Expulsion from the Garden of Eden	150
All the Time the Same	151

The Sirens Died Away	152
Signs	153
Cleopatra	154
A Line	155
Poesy	156
A Rooster Is Singing	157
We Are Mistaken	158
The Eyes	159
A Landscape	160
A Wall	161
At a Village Graveyard at the Wall of Self-Murderers	162
Encounter III	163
Eodem Anno Pons Ruptus Est	164
A Wall	165
The Death of a Poet	166
Eternity	167
A Suitcase	168
Have a Look	169
A Canvas	170
A Statuette	171
People	172
Gods Are ...	173
An Autumnal Night at a Lake	174
Nothingness	175
The Turk's Field	176
All the Time Again	177
A Danseuse	178
At a Cemetery	179
At a Wayside Cross	180
When I Breathed In the Scent	181
An Encounter IV	182

An Encounter V	183
They Are in a Hurry	184
She Asked You	185
Shrove Tuesday	186
A Vision	187
With the Least Attachment	188
Passing By	189
The Passion Week	190
Encounter VI	191
This Too	192
The Smiles	193
In the Very Morning	194
Lovers I	195
Rembrandt	196
At a Funeral	197
A Gramophone Record	198
Encounter VII	199
A Human Voice	200
An Evening Cloud	201
An Abyss of an Abyss	202
In the Kitchen	203
Two of Them	204
Encounter VII	205
Constructions for Eternity	206
When a Boy	207
She I	208
Everything	209
Lovers II	210
Like in a Film ...	211
They Told Him	212
In the Province	213

It Rained	214
A Village Noon	215
So	216
When	217
Per Procuram	218
At the Night of Amazement	219
A Sunday Afternoon at a Prague Suburb	220
An Expectation	221
Woman and Word	222
A Child	223
En Route	224
At a Rural Graveyard During the Village Wake	225
Minkowski's World	226
The End?	227
Eva II	228
At a Wedding	229
The Earth	230
Without a Funeral	231
Two Lives	232
Lovers III	233
A Countryside	234
Inside Out	235
Patient Dusk	236
A Winter Night	237
Sleeplessness	238
At the End of August	239
Legacy	240
October	241
From the Darkness	242
In Hell as Well	243
Before a Fig	244

Idols from the Cyclades	245
On the First Sunday in Lent	246
Anywhere I	247
Anytime in September	248
Dalila	249
Just to Step In	250
Melampygos	251
From the History I	252
A Hereditary One	253
Three	254
A Sound and a Footstep	255
Paraklit	256
Mezza Di Voce	257
Temptation	258
As in a Dream	259
Ice Is Cracking	260
A Storm in the Mountains	261
A Swan	262
Pelasgians	263
A Premonition	264
A Note	265
A Prison and a Sheepfold	266
Mother	267
A Still Life at a Lake	268
A Voice	269
From a Village	270
Clay	271
Hor	272
Verses	273
With a Knife into the Heart	274
Lovers IV	275
An Ancient Woman	276

An Ode	277
June	278
Night after Night	279
A Testimony	280
The Rope Ladder	281
From History II	282
Yes or No?	283
Life II	284
Stay with Me	285
Anywhere II	286
Moses	287
Clarity	288
Spiritual Retreat	289
It Does not Have to Be, But	290
When Listening to a Gramophone Record	291
The Star for One Second Only	292
Always ahead Of	293
For Everyone	294
A Saint	295
An Atom	296
An Epoch	297
Along the Way	298
She II	299
A Confession	300
Already Now	301
Yes	302
On the Advance	304

Introduction
by Dr Jiří Brabec
(Czech literary critic and historian)

Nothing can excuse a poet ...

Nothing can excuse a poet, not even his death.
And yet, from his hazardous existence,
a few signs always remain,
somewhat in excess. And in these,
certainly not any perfection, even if it were Paradise,
but truthfulness, even if it should be Hell ...
                              (On the Advance)

The poems collected in this book, *Yet There is Music,* are
the entirety of Holan's lyrics from the period of 1939-1948,
although only published in book form well after that
time. The first part, *Without a Title,* appeared in 1963, and
the second part, *On the Advance,* one year later. During
the years between the completion of the book and the
publication of its first part, Holan's poetry was listed in
the Communist index of forbidden books. Only a few of
his older works were re-edited, and only three bibliophile
editions of some new works were published. The ideological
aversion of Communist officials was chiefly pointed at his
lyrics, the complex form of which was perceived by them as
an offence.

For Holan, the lyrics were always a realm for questioning the sense of human existence—the mystery of human existence in the world. The verses in *Yet There is Music* are often perceived as if they were written under the shadow of the books that Holan was publishing at that time. Those were lyric-epic compositions, directly relating to the "mad epoch" of World War II: *Dream (1939)* and *The First Testament (1940)*; the epic images of fatal human tragedies, *Terezka Planetova (1943)* and *The Trail of a Cloud (1945)*; and the post-war pamphlet poetry, *To You (1947)*, and the portraits of simple Soviet soldiers in *Red Army Soldiers (1946)*. These works, which found a large number of readers and placed Holan among the most eminent European poets, led readers, however, into a too-simplified conception of the author, who seemed to have abandoned the reflexive poetry in which he used to attempt to give names to multivalued and elusive images of an abysmal "fervour of existence". Holan, however, never abandoned the domain in which a concrete moment blends with existential questions. It is *Yet There is Music*, therefore, that can put the finishing touches to our comprehension of the astonishing breadth of the poet's poetics.

The two citations which Holan uses as epigraphs are characteristic of his lyrics. The English poet Percy Bysshe Shelley is the author of the first epigraph, "Lost angel of a ruined paradise", from his *Adonais*. The second, from the English astrophysicist Sir Arthur Stanley Eddington, presents the question, "What if our universe came into existence from the ruins of something that was here before it ...". In the first poems of this collection, the words resound – "nothing to begin with", as supporting the notion of the emptiness of human existence. Human existence is marked by the dubiousness of its any raison-d'être whatsoever. A human being lives in a world of nothingness, in a void. The consciousness of the instability of the godless world, the impossibility of anchoring human existence, the ambiguity and delusiveness of all phenomena that surround humans—all lead Holan to the question: "Are we apostates, or castaways?". This question resounds in other images as well: "We come from ruins, with love besmeared ...", "The haste looking under its masks to find again and again its lost future." Holan's richly metaphorical poetry revolves around these verses. Holan himself succinctly conveyed his poetics: "– the picture / that is not an abyss here / can't be a sign." His poetry reveals the drama of a poet led by a time of crises and wars into the abyss of human existence.

Holan's poetic reflection is spread among images saturated by concrete events and incidents, evoking a multilayered course of events of a sensuously grasped world and, on the abstract level, bequeathing that "thievery of senses" to the level of false fiction. From this point of view, the first lines of many poems are truly significant. For example: "It's not long ago when I met in the street an unknown girl", or "I remember well: it was a beautiful
summer day / around noon ...", or "He came to me just when we were arriving / at the last tram stop ...". The starting point of Holan's verses is a concrete event, scene, experience, or recollection which shifts soon to the level

of a symbolic actuality. Aside from meditations, arising directly from the concrete, we come across scenes of fractions of reality, fragments seemingly wrung from the stream of events, and with the descriptions of situations of marginal character, in the midst of which the fate of humans plays out. Holan's literary production is rich in semantic shifts, paradoxes, oxymora, allegories, changes in contrast, time overlaps, abrupt changes of subjects, and diffusion of symbolic and non-symbolic zones. It is a dialogic poetry: not by chance, there are eight poems with the title Encounter in this book where an actor almost always speaks, giving the poet's expression dynamism.

Holan does not distinguish between great and small themes; all events and signs lead to the experience of a human who seeks in vain among them for a centre and a focus of his life. He forces the words to bear witness to the relationships and connections in which humans are destined to live and die. The obstinacy with which he plumbs the individual images of human lives is another testimony of his fascination with the eternal fight, without end and without any repose. The bitter awareness is always present, as in his lines: "We have never been the whole. We have only resembled, / but resembled to the full. / Now, when we begin to become an aggregate, / we try ourselves only as a portion of our likeness, / which, in the future, we shall totally leave. / What may become of us?"

As the author entitled this poem "An Epoch", he then offered the reader one of the keys to his work, in which the dread of the void is accompanied, even if only slightly, by a faith in discovering a purposeful life. In *On the Advance*, too, there are verses in which Holan uses light appearing in the midst of shadows, as if the way towards a fuller, ampler, more integral humanity was not lost forever: "O life – yes, you! Still only you! / You, in a friendly conversation and a kindly shaken hand, / you, in the deeds of good will because of heart's hope ...".

The book of lyrics that followed *Yet there is music* has the eloquent title *Dolour*. It was written in the fifties, the years of Holan's self-imposed seclusion. And it is exactly in these texts that Holan presents himself again as a poet of woes and the poverty of humans, who live in the times of a total "non-safeguarding".

> Translator's note: On May 17, 2010, Dr Jiří Brabec received the most prestigious Czech F.X. Šalda Prize for literary criticis

WITHOUT A TITLE

To Jan Řezáč

*A form is your pretense
to lead with and be led ...
Yet life's quintessence
is formless lead.*

*Inbreathing life's glow,
your wishes came full force ...
Abandon them all
and seek your source.*

*Of things, large or small,
you are full of thought ...
But God, after all,
fits into nought!*

I   **NOTHING TO BEGIN WITH**

The morgue fattens up to a shadow ... And boys
are knocking down plums with bones.
That dual fall with a second-to-none sunstroke
blink briefly through a half-closed ear of vertigo
and then let all the colours die out
into the graveyard's negritude.

Nothing to begin with. Only
the first end with the second one
expectorates the blood of music
upon the palm lines, which have
a mere year of space
behind the cracks of walls.

II DISCERNMENT

If life floats along the stream
and death against the stream –
we cannot discern its mouth.

If life floats against the stream
and death along the stream –
we cannot discern its source.

III   WHY?

Because God's voice
is a mere surface of silence
under the oppression of our ear –
why then should things be forever
a hard-of-hearing amalgam of a mirror,
into which our stipulation looks?

IV SWELTER

Exalted blaze crawls like an eagle
that would have a dog's qualms ...

Amorphous agony of bliss
with trust in nothingness – not harbouring the former –
winds its way up, with its hundred mouths,
along both sides of blood.

Feeling can contrive more than a feeling
only with a serpent's grace ...
But God, at the water's edge, keeps His nakedness
upon the angels of the desert.

v LIKE NO ONE

"No, for years now I've had nothing to do with you!"
He says it almost disdainfully.
He does not confide. Barely is he eager
to explain whether he intends to hurt
or, unexpectedly, make up his mind.
Oh, he is like no one who resists
speaking for anyone,
and his three hundred limbs confuse
the invisibility that can be heard
in a primordial sense of touch, marvelling
that his dress, too, has been taken
in reasonable instalments at the Essential's ...

Look, an angel – an angel-beginner –
but already an angel-cognomen:
a deserter or a spy!

VI A PICTURE THAT IS NOT AN ABYSS

Under a linden tree, a saint's beard is dyed ...

The ignorant air quivers
with the virginity in the ears of a graveyard.
The blush happens without itself;
the girls' laugh quits hold of their nakedness –
and the scent,
while shining only because becoming extinct,
denies that singing
could have a man only with a stone.

And yet, and yet: the picture
that is not an abyss here
can't be a sign.

VII   A TRIPTYCH

Even if we may outpace our consciousness,
our inspiration stands in our light ...

The dead, they are indeed space.

VIII A FUNERAL

Behind a graveyard wall,
from a coffin you stare
at rental deeds' free fall,
leaves in the air.

The rain ascends ... The air
is now wet to its core.
You leave. They play fanfare
to angels' lore.

Behind a graveyard wall,
they play a tune to graves.
You clear out Miser's Hall
for Grinner's Place.

IX   YET

Show me a single smile devoid of mystery,
and I explain to you what suffering is.
Show me a single tear devoid of mystery,
and I surmise what joy is ...

Yet mere desire for it would have to be
a question without an earthly tongue.

x   PERUSING SHELLEY'S LETTERS

Bliss is not in a brimful heart ...

Though exactly then, when
a smoky outreach of delights resounds up to the cavernous
repercussions of sadness,
a thought wishes a tomb for its pillars.

If water really flows,
then a free and consolatory quietude
hardly resides in repose.

And a poet? Look here, he goes,
goes – like not alive anymore – somewhere else,
if he is still to be here ...

XI ECSTASY

Nature that should take wing to God
would have to renounce the one in all:
one being in all beings, one fruit in all fruits.

To man, it is enough to find nadir.

XII IN THE RUINS

Presence? Presence of what?

A horse, contained by the hand of colours,
does not flee, not even at night,
yet those boulders, and that force,
in the hairs of cracks!

Look: a temple, the temple of Hera, Zeus, Baal-Hadad!
The sex of their death had no ovaries
for moving the pillars ...

XIII **TODAY**

Look here, you, who perfumes the lea,
and, before you kiss, you secretly
wet your cracked lips –
how hereafterly and silently

a butterfly, landing on your hand to stay,
stretches her wings out and in,
like the lungs of those flowers
you've plucked off today!

XIV NOT ONLY QUALMS

They have only one tooth and one eye,
and they lend them to each other like the old Graiai did
    once.
And, like them, they temper with forebodings
within an analyzing trance.

When silence, under pressure of a tear, changes its shape,
they ask for details of night scenes.
And you feel how they are stretching out
like parchment in wetted screens.

Between supine nature and vertical spirit,
they are the beauty, dancing on a snake with ease ...
Even the satanizing energy of the sleep
has something of Eden – of Eden to appease.

xv A SLEEPING ONE
to Vladimír Justl

When tears roll down eyelashes' lair,
a girl sleeps ... She sleeps and purrs.
The forest bites into her hair
with golden teeth of prickly furze ...

It won't let go. And not today,
when the sun falls to a dim yell,
as if a dog, sightless and stray,
threw up a wedding ring to hell.

What were once forms and shapes to trim
may now fill up the Universe.
Fear streams along her every limb,
the fear of excess to disperse.

Look at the hissing juggernaut,
kissing her breasts, now left, now right ...
She's pale and bloodstained, as if caught
in bed sheets on her wedding night.

And her delusive fantasy
has destroyed all that's faint today ...
Her soul has more souls than you may see
in one body ever to stay.

But soon a shaking whitish hue
touches with darkness its own skin ...

More of her bodies come in view
for just one soul of just one kin.

xvi TO HAVE

What else to want from abstract names
than overcrowded cells of moans,
when every item says: no claims! –
and you obey them to have what it owns.

Are we just streams that gnaw and totter?
Are we asked to be earth and stone?
A stream must, it must ... But the water
owns sans ever owning its own.

XVII A SNAKE

Along a rocky footpath walks a man
with a handful of snakes ...
A hiss, as light as a feather, somewhat coiled,
thrills the air and the consanguineous
rebounding minutes
into the glitter of the cerebral world beyond,
in front of which the sun clasps
the pupil of our feeling ...

Not otherwise, but with a gloomy energy
the snake of the spinal cord always cajoles woman,
and lust hungers only for a prolonged moment,
as if it wanted to become hate
even after death – – –

He who intrudes, imprisons ... And he imprisons himself ...
The boulders of burial mounds
are returned to the egg by their gradual relief,
in which concealed interrogation waits only for the world
until it won't last to the morrow of delusions.

A footstep of a man died away ... But the menace –
left over without reserve and wide open
to a more bearable quiver –
has, in fact, already condemned ...

Are we apostates, or castaways?

XVIII   OUT OF LOVELESSNESS

Despite a touch of radiance,
darkness always has the last word.
We come from ruins, with love besmeared ...

But Lumerpa, that shining bird,
who so strongly outshone all lights
that his own shadow disappeared!

xix DEEP IN THE WOODS

Just slightly longer air, and it lacks some modesty ...
But here only steam, like the force
chased out of horses into the woods,
snuffs at its image in an undertone.

Around magic, the world assaults
the verdure with a somewhat heartless tenderness;
anguish feels warmer only below nothing
whereto every cunning sound
lets the thievery of senses drain away –
and in front of stones,
the little soul of a pattering moment
feels for the past life of primroses ...

Nature, in the masculine breed of silence,
has not just itself.
So, did somebody once walk through this depth?
Starting, changing himself, and enticed, must he go on,
always too early with regard to augury?

Nothing here talks about him. Only a non-trace.
But this very one: how it pleads, cries, engraves itself and
    wanes
near the octopus of a tree stump!

xx NO

A journey is to be abandoned, not to be seen.
Both a tower and a bloom are no allegory,
and an image unmasked the entire mien.

You of course say: See! And you make a story
out of all that guards its spring with sun screen.

How is the green to be warm and mellow,
as it is no tree, no oak, no sallow?

xxi A BITTER ONE

No, don't kiss my hand, my beloved, stay lying!
Your dress, heard through every one of your movements,
keeps dead women with me ...

After the convergence of all senses into that point
where passion wanted only prolongation,
every present moment is an ash grey-eyed
dyad of the soulless air –
close your black-spots, don't look for me!

In the pain of cognition, there is still enough emptiness
for a bitter non-secular love ...

XXII ALL THE TIME

Always that haste that hardly asks:
"To strive with a wound? Or to decide?"
The haste looking under its masks
to find again and again its lost future.

The haste that escaped eternity:
a man's inhaling and a woman's exhaling
can never push any appearance away,
and their fluidity only tails their stay
from one form to another.

The haste that is the extinction
more than once in a nonexistent snip ...
Look here! Even the horses of a hearse
are driven with a whip.

XXIII ONLY IN DARKNESS

The light is in the lower state of clouds.
Snow already creeps down.
The air combs its hair on the willows.
The earth is retrospecting. The fountains are surmising.
For the love of life, even a crow
flies past without any sound,
and a seed too is lacking words...

But not all that's silent is mute.
The cave at the left hand's knoll is very calm.
And if it soon fills up with soldiers,
it will be because of some chatterer.
Homer, in front of the vulva of a Trojan mare in foal...

XXIV   AN EVENING IN MAY

An evening in May ... A scent that's menacing ...
Prostitutes under me and holes in the rocks.
Darkness echoes darkness.

Even the monument in my bed is of flesh and blood.
The clothes are left behind.
Delight almost mine ... But death
discerns it ...

Lilac, laden into turkeys' wattles,
gobbles ...

xxv WITHOUT A TITLE

He is afraid to lose what he is.
He is afraid to become God.
He resists by engorgement.
He hinders God to become man.

XXVI **WHEN?**

Carnal towns or mountains ...
How it trembles, there and here,
the void, sensitive enough
to favour absence
at the door of the world.

We ask: When? ... But this is no love.
And love itself is still not a soul.

XXVII IN THE GROVES OF THE CHLUMEC REGION

Insects rattle the air
with the metallic string of E.
If it breaks, it will tear
the eye of a tree.

And higher heights are sought
for a rising lust.
And then a wail ... A nought ...
a thrustless thrust.

The heat with no relief
retuned the summery chord.
The pool shields with a leaf
of lotus a pesky wart.

XXVIII A DUET

The Voice:

Only no bounds and passive ambition
will see him, if you don't discern.
He is not far. It is sufficient
to enter, for you who don't adjourn.

The Contra-voice:

He loves far lands and fights in fair play.
And of his river, he loves its ear's long lobe.
A spring at the sea, or not far away,
brings a brook, too short for something to probe.

xxix BY TRAIN

A whistle-stop in a valley. Look: a piece of masonry,
and, like years ago, it still welts here
that tree of beer, the chestnut tree.
And like then, all is only third
of scary sounds that have their knives ready.
The penis of a horse turned up his sleeve.
The rain in the door feels womanlike already.
A castle in ruins, like a hit to your breast,
and the same air that won't live any further ...

But what I miss here is the child that drove out flowers
from the railway station garden
to the graveyard of its grandfather.

xxx SUBIDAS I

The pulse knocks on the body walls
some stipulated signs.
Imprisoned, we know what each one wants,
we too want all that sounds.

Yet somewhere alone, with no calls
from angels, days and nights –

a saint's breath, full of fire,
knows how to break through any ring.
He destroys his desire
before he's destroyed by suffering.

XXXI A FLYLEAF

Into the world, it rains and gleams.
To be, though, contradicts the fall.
The past world plays with umpteen themes,
but back there, God doesn't speak at all.

Walk in your reason from life's glow
straight into an autumnal frost,
so your poem and tongue will grow
like grapes, their sweetness never lost.

Never can we be what we are to be.
Indeed, if we were to become man,
we would have to create ourselves. But then,
this is already the might of God.

You lost all, being kissed by him.
He bequeathed you a brutish scheme.
But all that embellishes you
you'll get back, if it's kissed by you.

XXXII LOVERS

Do we go on or rather stay, my beloved?
Look, how everything inheres and cruelly persuades
that the way to our house that found itself
leads nowhere.

Simple and persuasive is a tree,
and a stone in the fields suggests to you that the statue
is all the time someone else, somewhere else,
and, therefore, as the divine one, it is allowed to stay here.

It's not so long, when we were standing at this place,
blissful in our love by the anguish of suspense,
which used to pull down into rapture
even the roughest reality.

It's not so long, when we lived in our kissing lips,
believing into inarticulateness of all tongues,
and with pain not too much slavish
for finding its relief in defiance ...

Today, both of us shelterless, we carry in our little bundle
bread of ergot and wine of angel's trumpet,
listening to the dead how they walk
one over the other, in graveyard's caterpillars.

XXXIII **SUBIDAS II**

You'll see nothing until you have turned blind
to heady nights of a miraculous design.
A cellar? You will not find
if you have not looked for wine.

You'll never reach the godsent eloquence
that gives the first note to an inspired theme
if you feared an unforeseen sentience:
– and did not fear it with a sweet gleam!

xxxiv **FATE**

It is only a little mountain path through the woods ...
Even if clouds come around
to consciousness of heavens
and illuminate it for a short while,
you feel that its solitude
was once chosen by darksome mournfulness.

Stop your steps here! ... Be silent! ... And meditate!
You have barely more than that path:
a stone for your life and an edifice for your death.

xxxv AT A FERRY

Rustling trees, and rocks, and waves ...
Everything, that exists and lives, desires
to unify all that's real
by some imaginary difference.

But not the waves, it's we who feel unsure,
be it as lovers, or as mortals –
because the voice of forms decides by itself
the silence of a transformation.

We may even not exist. And only a genius and an assassin
extract their irrevocability
even from some secondary course of events.

XXXVI REAL LIFE

Not that with God we dispute!
We inhibit his forcefulness!
Woe to us who are in pursuit
of what we ourselves exude.

Thus self-imprisoned in our deeds,
we take our shackles as an ornament,
not understanding that games
are both the fundament
and the peak of the Universe.

XXXVII AS IT'S IN THE BOOKS

As it's in the books: the moon,
the autumn and red deer.
Noiseless is a woodpecker's tune
about the green one can't hear.

You walk wide open, and still
suddenly full of doubt
about the enormous thrill
of things that were dreamed out.

XXXVIII   **A NIGHT IN CERNOHOUSY**

The whole night they carted wormwood
and shook the wall
under all appearances of sleeplessness.

A twinkling candle diffusively wrinkled
some accidental moments of tranquillity,
especially when the afterthought
blended with the word
into a rhythmical failure of an owl.

Every sound might have to concentrate,
if darkness had only its childhood in the space,
until it announced, destitutely constrained:
those who are outside are busy!

And they hastened ... The storm-hen
was slowly opening up
above the castle's tower –
and the lightning was a mere proof
that the preponderance of observation without love
goes for the images with a knife ...

With every squeal of the farm wagons
you felt that, whatever everywhere else,
the beds of those in limbo were squeaking with the future –
and you, infelicitous, asked
where such birth can be
in which you could find more than some primeval awe ...

xxxix   THE AUTUMN IN THE MOUNTAINS

It's autumn ... My beloved is far away
and a voice has ended within her light
under the surface of a stone ...

Is detachment a nearness? What do we know about an
    encounter?
How mysteriously the memory
of her not-yet-kissed breast quivers,
but also joy, as incomprehensible
as the last words of the dying ones!

It is with tears that the vision of desire comprehends
a lakeside flash in the marrow of herons,
and a tree knows well that to give away
means to give back,

and you yourself are nothing but the feeling
that destitution without emptiness
has either buried its abyss
or has not found it yet.

XL EVEN IF

It was piously yearned,
a dream, epic and pure,
satisfied at the end:
yielding to a female lure.

All that's superior
abandons every lane.
It's the infernal core
that staunchly clings to man.

XLI THE VILLAGE SPRING

He who guards what's been planted
knows more intimately the underworld.
Not in the least is he terrified by the powers outside this world,
nor by some bottomless waft, heaved up when the leaves
in the book of the dead were turned over,
nor when the harmony of ideas is in accord with a non-word ...
He forefeels the confluence of limbs with polytheism;
he hears roosters, and the echo of their voice
resounds in their testicles;
he perceives the blissful movement of trees in the caves
– and if he appears in front of the Reaper's measure,
he feels no horror because
it is the dialect of graves
in which the earth is talking to him ...

XLII A WATERFALL

He who is in the valley and still hesitates
whether to reach for a tumbler –
he would have already been a drunkard here.

A gently sounding stream, that shy rumbler,
always softens more, whenever it rather
admits that a bluish-grey red dogwood, too,
quivers with fear ...

Someone asks: "What are the sources?"
And a poet says, as you may hear:
"The mountains recognized each other."

XLIII   **THE BRIDGE ACROSS THE RIVER L.**

After woods in writing, the land under the bridge
is fully verbal.
Nothing can silence its waves,
nothing our gloomy farewell.

Your hands, numb with cold, move me to tears,
the sun in the clouds too,
while choking, sobbing, turning red
like a child in a knacker's pocket.

And a serious hour coaxes
with its evil eye!
Which can be stronger: your
fatality or irreparability?

Because he once loved without warning,
precisely that most gentle of all feelings
does not want to be protected,
wide open to everything, nude up to death.

How innumerably black affinities
can change any remorse!
Nothing is more fertile than the cruel
carnal power of a distressed source ...

XLIV AN EVENING AT INDIAN SUMMER

The moon, tired of rocks and brooks,
is dressed up in black lingeries.
A red cloud fails to change the looks
of raspberries to blackberries.

Naught to drink, and the days draw in.
The light shines more only in grapes,
and crickets work with so much din,
hammering rails to autumn days.

XLV AT A GRAVEYARD

So this is to be that door without a house?
Close it silently, walk silently in,
and, suddenly freer, notice
how fully alive is your melancholy
that the slightest suggestion of a cypress tree
takes it aback.

An unaccounted reconciliation strengthens slowly from above,
and worldly excitement sizzles only through a moment,
like a little wick of a candle, squeezed by a wetted finger,
yet it does not disturb; it even flames out with a defiance almost
so that you move along
because even a godlike image is only a mere replacement of factuality.

A ferrous angel, who dries only in rainstorms,
could have a name if it were not a word already –
with rings on his feet and with a nest in his underarm,
he dreams against time on his own accord
as when a thought has had a scented headache for a long time ...

Simple is Fool's Parsley, Snapdragon, even Dyer's Litmus.
Warm is Mullein, tall to man's height of the moon.
The youth contains transience in every one of its looking up –
ah, how are you going to do it to stay this way,
yourself not at home for yourself, and not feeling
apparitions tragically fumbling about,
while the dividing line is in accord with a blind mind?

Ah, how are you going to do it? Say it, say it then,
you, who cannot begin anything
without going against oneself from the finality!
You, rather impatient to allow the pain
to stay in the created creating
for so long that you could catch up
with nothing but the future.

XLVI TWO LAKES

Wine is deeper than a cup.
Verdure has an eye for the evenings.
Silence among pillars disturbs the cries
of a roosting pheasant.

You dream (searching through your memories)
that it could be joy,
which, clean, would, by its play, tie up together
the other world with the world here.

And your memory slowly paints for you
how once charmed you beheld
a girl lying at a slender dyke
with her hands in two lakes.

XLVII   BEFORE A STORM

When all turned dark at a bubbling weir,
swooning blood understood it well
why foamy walls seemed queer
with hemlock's rabietic smell.

As if the wound was missing something,
something that healed, not losing its peace –
an inviting womb seems uninviting
when filled up with the strength of trees.

A woman bites herself into her lover's lips ...

XLVIII **VERSES**

The wave, where a fish plays music
from the memory of pebbles,
a graveyard wall on which nappies are dried,
a bird, a falling leaf, a voice somewhere in the fog –
they simplify every gesture,
despite that the pull of history through nature
erodes the images as far away as to our instincts.

Sorrow responds to the complicated hatefulness
as simply
as when a son
selects the finest words of murder –
and his mother wipes her tears with an apron.

XLIX **THE 31ST OF DECEMBER**

How every mania belongs to us!
As if the year poured wine into oats in the stable of
 months,
and as if windstorms were a measure
for inspiration, forgotten in a flash!
How every delight belongs to us,
worn away by the heart failure of a falling stone!
How every dying love belongs to us,
which, in despair, wants to renew eternity
that did not cease to be evanescence.

Even in distress, there is something final.
If you stayed alive, then only because
you have quickly created another ...

L   MEMORY OF A LUNAR NIGHT NEAR LIBOC

A close-lipped darkness was there as a breath
and as a transformation, the most powerful one
among the spirits of the earth.

Haze was allowed anything ... So you didn't even ask about
what had decided that a falling stone
took the side of the wind without the air.

Insularly moved to tears, you beheld
a couple of saintly madmen passing by ...
Their fate was silent inside them like a song
destined for lifelong concealment.

A song perceived by the body
works in a mirror.
And adolescence is nothing but a lover
for a while eyeless in a perpetual self-sightedness ...

LI A HOROSCOPE

An evenfall ... A graveyard ... And the wind, as sharp
as bony splinters at a butcher's block.
Rust shakes out its prototype from the form of scrapings.
And above all that, and above the tears of shame,
there is a star almost determined to confess
why we don't comprehend simplicity until our heart bursts,
suddenly bare, alone, and already without fate ...

LII   A SLEEPING BOY

On the moss, in the verdant breeze,
a boy sleeps, as undressed by June.
All around him are blackberries,
spilled like pellets of a loon.

Just above him, squirrels sharpen
the pencils of pines, one by one.
Look at wind's hand, wary and hempen,
how it paints his face with the sun.

How pale they are, black-and-gold nixies,
sucking his sweat, oh, what a sweet task:
each one like a wasp that soon affixes
its sting to fresh lacquer of his cask.

LIII   **RAPIDS AT THE RIVER OTAV**

When a stone is in love,
the stream is not sufficient to extinguish the thighs of
    a river.
But even passion moves only into a likeness,
hissing a great, blackishly confused errand.

An errand to whom? From whom? Being so subterranean
    and so airy
it might not be a burden even in a fall,
it ignites the flash powder of the unconscious inside
    mystery.

There is no "here". And there is no joy.
Radiance, the spoken one, has its mouth in the graves of
    sounds,
and you may feel what you feel, only one thing intrudes on
    you:
that man is not more
than an error made during the scrutiny of the dead.

LIV   **A SULTRY NIGHT**

Moon's hatred ... How much it strives
to weave from the otherworld's seams!
Even a dog has rabid Alps
on the glacier of its teeth.

Lovers, as cross as two sticks,
break dreamily each other's bone.
Admiringly their self-love peeks
in the graveyard's water well alone.

Soon a shadow will appear,
a streak at which bitches howl ...
What from graves is coming near
is a killer on the prowl.

LV   NO, DON'T GO YET

No, don't go yet, don't be scared by commotions.
It is a bear, opening up the beehives in the orchard.
He will quiet down soon. I too will conceal
my parlance, like the haste of the snake's semen
to the woman in Eden.

No, don't go yet, don't lower your veil.
The meadow flared up with the methylene of colchicums.
It is you, after all, life, even if you mean:
– Desiring, we attach. But love
is solely itself ...

LVI   ALONG A STREET

Both blood and bile are black, and even tears are cloudy;
time of senses turned into ravens to grate their phantoms;
breath helps itself from its death-robe;
the sledge of grief hovers and looks for what could be
    polluted;
the darkness smokes inside fates and writes its preview
    with a charcoal
when someone's voice – "I too wish to be burned,
but by nettles behind the crematorium" –
illuminates both a shadow and a feel, and the speechless
    earth ...

LVII **YOU, WOMAN**

The rain in the window prints
upon your debauchery
a few bulbs of hyacinths,
cracked like a swan's lechery.

You give up, darkishly disguised
like a dream devoured by a dream.
The houses, as you have surmised,
are inside a threshold's rim.

Your hips in heat, a pair of tongs
pull your lover down to godlike spheres,
while death tells you about your wrongs
from the lines on your heels.

LVIII **A MOMENT**

This is that moment: music cannot
and the word does not want ... a gloomy null line,
drawn by breath, indicates avidly
that the whole reality is needed,
if a deed is to become an image ...

It starts to rain ... Dahlias' riddle comes off ...
A murderer at a well washes his hands.

LIX   THE NOON

Glint looses hair of a sylvan scent.
And in lines of no heights,
resound the hues well fed and spent
as to notice nuns' flights.

Gravestone's pulse knows to loom the black
and, with darkness, to allure
when a shirt sticks firm to the back,
sweated by a paramour.

Nature, living from what's not alive,
is a point, a loop, a flare.
But we, even amidst what our hearts contrive,
remain unaware.

LX   I WONDER IF YOU RECALL

I wonder if you recall, you, whom the feet of magic
once brought to me, how to us nothing was enough
to tie firmly all our embraces
with the knot of our passion?
Which of us noticed that in the meantime
the bridge was pushing away incessantly both banks,
that love's agreement with violence
was already preparing for each of us
a delusive lie-death, blown-off promises,
mirrors, rollicking with the haste of images,
and all the faraway lands, arisen from disdain,
where fright itself blasphemes twice along its rim?

Only the hands of God are isolated
by such a huge space
that they seem to be clasped ...

LXI **THERE ARE THE SEAS**

Grief can't be wasted away
even with a child.
Alone you must wake and wake
when the dark is beguiled.

Your hand won't move the switch
wherever it appears.
There are the seas you reach
only in tears.

LXII OH WE, WE DISGRACED?

O we, we disgraced! But what power when a recluse,
mortally without his body, spiritually without any measure,
still pungently forced himself
into a shirt made of the hair of whores
and drank only the snow that melted in front of a bawdy
    house –
while God was in a female abyss,
as far as bliss from female saints!
O we, we disgraced?

LXIII   TIME GRATES ITS TEETH

Time grates its teeth and roars,
while starting to affirm
that all that pours and pours
is the dust of a woodworm.

The whip of storms marauds
the trees with raging gust.
It is the first of drops
the tempest weds with dust.

Through heath that moans and groans,
along a flogging track,
a Czech woman goes,
a coffin on her back.

Time grates its teeth and roars,
and the moon, self-confined,
into your tears it pours
sleeping pills for your night ...

LXIV A STORM AT THE RIVER

A sooty gust of clouds bleakly covered
the wick of sunshine and the battered enamel of heavens.
Fear grows older where children, not long ago,
spewed out into each others mouths a willow leaf,
and where glitter may have a look as black as twelve nights.

Just in passing, I touched your young breast,
just lightly water laid its finger on a wave –
and a rhythm, as long as courting goes,
discovers elements while looking for harmony ...

LXV SOMNIA ET NOCTIUM PHANTASMATA

This is the night when apparitions of excessive creation
enter through the secret door of a vigil
in order to succumb to their demise.
A doorstep gives a bitterly creaky sound, and some robes wait
in their extinct concentration, which sparkles up
the time schedule according to an owl –
some trait takes pains in vain
to become a smile without a transfiguration of the heart –
some hand thinks in echoes
of the voice combed over the ears of limbo –
some steps resound with hesitation only,
(besides, the future is for them a must,
yet this very same does not want them) –
when suddenly one shadow persuasively bends down
to burn a little crust of stigmata
in the little flame of the Eternal light
till all eyes are watching it ...

Only you are still asleep, rather wilfully,
as if you were to surmise,
by longhaired lingering in the coffin,
the shuttered comb of an angel.

LXVI **A STROLL**

The circle of the horizon was cold
like squatting at the stove of an almshouse ...
A friend turned after a drop of sound,
which was skidding along the goat's hair of mythology.
We returned ... A small waterfall
modelled itself by the wetness
like a woman's belly at the washtub.

LXVII   **A DUET II**

The Voice:

Things and names and pale forbearance.
Few fine nets and some rough fencing.
A stance, that's motion. Why that riddance
of solitude for lonely sensing?

The Contra-voice:

To abandon and feel Eden
means much more than defiance.
Nearness is a blissful leaven.
But divorce – a charming faience.

LXVIII **DIALOG**

Today, when standing near a cavern
that drank some waves with its dark muscle,
you asked me, meaning evanescence:
"What does a stream tell men?"

– A stream? As if eating the sphinx's marrow,
he mumbled to us through the darkness:
What does not stop at our waistline,
won't be a woman inside its head.

LXIX   **BEHIND**

Through dusk, less and less soothing,
the moments walk their pace.
How could a tally count something,
if it's a fading face?

There are answers which tempt
behind the space of daylight.
What's a wall to a saint?
Only for standing upright ...

LXX   BUT THERE IS WINE

He who makes distinctions becomes human
and understands only the mortal one ...

But there is wine ... Inside its mystery
ancient poets used to forget
how a reason with no groves and no snow
was to punish the trail of the foxes.
Not the least did a raven terrify them, who flew
the accreted eyebrow of a funeral,
not the least were they perturbed by the cries of an infant,
not the least were they confused by pellucid simplicity of
    cruel suffering,
which often hinders vision in the thoughts.

And if a man has a woman in his middle
on both sides of the nature,
then they decided for nothing
unified, in the very point of God, with everything.

LXXI SUFFERING

In the deceptive air and with a gloomy ruin
of a cloud in the background: a reaper hones his scythe
as if effacing primeval smudges on the walls of Egbatan
with the soft insides of a loaf.

Favourably native fruit is not for us after all,
and hardly can any spirituality set us at ease.
Even perfect attachment still knows suffering,
indeed the suffering turned familiar with the dead who
    confide.

LXXII ETERNO NÒ, MA BEN ANTICO

Beauty and time ... Can, in truth, any
later destruction happen earlier
by only the composition and the growth in the one who
    loves?

It is always the same dazzlement in deeds.
What may it palpate but earth?

LXXIII   ALL THE TIME

The time that wrests and wrests
along with death-knell toll ...
Even gods of the underground
don't let us extol.

The heavy weight of their heels
tears our muscles and breath.
It's the steady fall one hears
of those alive and those in death ...

LXXIV AT THE GRAVE OF K. H. MACHA

To be determined by one's body
has as well its own cast,
and in this way many a man found his land for himself,
he the earth at large and, before long, simply loam.

But you, the poet, you, young in your future,
young by your uninherited vision,
you yourself revealed it to yourself, knowing
that all the counter-void was needed
if an image was to become a feat.

Ah, what was time but cinders of phantoms,
flown down from the algebraic blackness of heavens
into the explosives, hidden in your pensive mood,
a May thunder, which bitterly illuminated for you
what gods were dissolving with their cruel drivel
upon the tongue of tragedy!

Fates, blood, and laughter and a ravenlike reticence,
when the flesh learns from hate
how much it loves its self-beast;
the black centre of longing, farewells outgrown
from the great allowed-to-be up to must-aversions;

the very human breath,
mindful in every foreign tongue
that, after a coffin, there is one tongue,
but also faithfulness, anointed by your suffering
for other souls –
how little they meant to you, perhaps only because
you, not willing to guard the tree as it was,
you plucked the fruits in their primeval existence! ...

And perhaps not death and a dream and a word,
which make everything even more enigmatic
as if mystery wanted to persuade us –
but a non-world now, conceived
by the sex of a genius and eternity,
called you like its son
and lured you away from this land,
where anger still
would be the most gloomy respite
if dolour were not here so free ...

A form. A living form. Alive enough or not.
But how mortal it is, though rising to touch the stars!
If God exists in an uncreated nought,
He is not present in the arts.

ON THE ADVANCE

To Angelo Maria Ripellino

Lost angel of a ruined paradise.

SHELLEY, Adonais

*What if our universe came into existence
from the ruins of something that was here before it ...*

SIR ARTHUR EDDINGTON

AFTER THAT, NOTHING

It dawns already and I don't know
why I've been rushing the whole week
from cold remoteness to this door
and now stand here before my time ...

I've not wanted to press the future,
nor to awaken the blind man.
He'll come to open it for me,
but he will be compelled to turn back ...

THE PRAYER OF A STONE

Paleostom bezjazy,
madžnín at kraun at tathău at saün
luharam amu-amu dahr!
Ma yana zinsizi?
Gamchabatmy! Darsk ādōn darsk bameuz.
Voskresajet at maimo šargiz-duz,
chisoh ver gend ver sabur-sabur.
Theglathfalasar,
bezjamy munay! Dana! Gamchabatmy!

WHO KNOWS

Mountains during a rain are one of the indications
of parched refinement.
But who knows whether being sought
like a shadow during harvest time
is not just a wilted leaf we hear,
or a too-old book we are browsing through,
or a cranial seam of the lightning we remember,
and whether it is not in the future where it rains ...

NEAR A FOOTPATH

It is an old woman selling newspapers
who hobbles up here every day ...
When, tired and unable to bear,
she unloads her bundle of "special editions",
sits down on it and then falls asleep ...
Those who walk along here
have become so accustomed to her
that they don't see her any more –
and she, mysterious and mute as a pythoness,
makes invisible what she should be hawking.

It begins to rain ...

WE KNOW NO ENDS, NO BOUNDS

It may be that time is preceding us
and, with a jagged validity,
impairs a little of everything
that we destroy by our blind love ...
A beam of light, run over by a cart,
was, a little earlier, trampled by the horse ...
But, maybe not.

AN EVENING IN A VILLAGE

Why this anxiety? Why these flashbacks,
attacking and gripping?
Why is every glancing up returned
with a sealed promissory note?
Why does the water take all footbridges?
Why does the only possible prophecy
always glance like the teeth of a night patrol?

Darkness at the borderline ... After he's crossed
    the graveyard,
the bell ringer climbs the stairs,
and, while he rings out the vesper bell,
boys, laughing, pile up
the tower entrance
with old gravestones.

REFLECTION?

Awoken at night, I sighted through the open window
two moons in the sky,
and, full of fear, I told myself:
The Judgement Day has come.
At once I felt so alone
that I didn't have time even for my loneliness,
the stomach of its childhood rising.
I felt so pathetic that even time,
which, at one time, was hiding
among the poems just written by me,
and thus once wanted their death,
didn't insist now on its own might.

O vanity! I was so unprepared
that I was, like a phantom, touching simple things
from each side of the ages,
as if the search could still be the future,
or maybe already only because
of that mute soliloquy,
which, obedient to an underground beat,
was throwing my soul from nothing to nothing ...

But, after a while, the wind closed the window a little,
and, at the sky, only one moon was standing there ...
The Judgement Day lies still ahead.

THE NIGHT BEFORE EVENING

A stab into the finger of a girlish age
has refused inside you any monumental grins of peepholes
for an earwig withdrawing into the ear of a statue,
for the sex of a premonition you may hear,
for cracked fruit on fertile feet of bliss.

Bitten by the lurking spinal chord of a groove,
you began as an *objet trouvé*,
which was wearily looking for Eve's notch
and the knocking down ...

ENCOUNTER I

Where is that little girl going?
With parting of her fine hair
in instalments of torn-out earrings,
with her school report for the first term of slighting,
and with little clogs soled by a coffin –
she wanders from the blind sex of an unfamiliar song
towards some still distant, ruthless,
spiteful night of seeds
along the cruel dry land of human feelings.

Even the very God himself has only tattooed ships ...

LAMENT OF ONE DECEASED

I was allowed to return for a while to my kindred.
Because it was my native province,
the boat-hire place was familiar to me,
and I soon arrived at the village.
The wind was helping the air into the sleeves of a weeping
   willow.
It was Sunday, my family was sitting in the orchard,
and only my sister was coming out from the cellar with
   some milk.
It never occurred to me that I could scare them.
But when they didn't believe that it was really I,
I shouldn't have told them that I was alive.
Everything scattered into thin air
with violet and daisy outcries,
and, in front of me, a cobwebbed landscape was crumbling,
and mezereon and moonlight and an alarm clock
atop a graveyard wall ...

WHILE WET

It is an autumnal rain, pig-headed ad nauseam,
which is collecting the foam of fury,
kept back by all the people
who have been locked in a chamber for a long time now.
Rather pale, they stand at the windows
and, with an immodest, snappish delight,
observe how, near a park, a drenched child
is offering paper flowers to no one there,
protecting them with the little hollow of her palm ...
She is protecting them in vain ... In vain is she offering ...
And in vain will she protect and offer them,
as long as she won't try it in the tongue of beasts,
or as long as she won't decide to go
into a park, spurned in an accentuated way,
where there is nothing but a little bench,
unplaned, without any paint,
a little bench, of which they were penny-wise,
the bench for the dead ...

BUT NEVER DOUBT I LOVE

A water rat, at the breast of drowned Ophelia,
grieving over the bruises and the scent void of any
    complexion,
squeals, sighs, kicks up its heels, talks through its nose,
and drops down its touching snuffles
along the globular acronyms of spit
to its rumble, jealous of the stream of the river,
when, suddenly, it sees a bluebottle at the belly of the
    drowned.
Immediately, it runs there, and begins to tear
the musty skin, which gives up easily;
it gnaws and tears and sucks; it bites, robs and gobbles;
it tastes the submersible draughts;
it mauls and plucks up some finer sheepish veins;
it eats through, criss-cross,
and, dribbling, it rinses down from little pools
concealed there by sickly rags, scrubby wraps
and shameless clouds of tissues and membranes,
aglow as its smacking;
it crams the flesh from the front into all the ends
    of consciousness,
and it thickens all around and turns heavy in its bulbous
    baldness ...
But, look, how it turns offensively distrustful,
and, watchful, glazes its left eye,
as, in that dissected maw of life,
a little body of a baby appears ...

YOU WALKED BY

It is a woeful, suburban skating rink,
poured over by a Christmas Eve spoon,
and frozen at the Epiphany ...
In one of its corners, an old fellow plays a gramophone.
Having only one record, he turns it again and again,
blowing off, with utmost gentleness, the snow from its
    surface
and carefully launching its tune,
which shivers like a mare before mating,
or like golden foils of countless duplicity,
which would be interrogated, each one separately,
by something that turned rusty long ago ...

All the appearance of the old fellow is like coming out from
    a vault,
but, at the same time, protruding
as if keeping his clothes in the loft;
he turns the same record all the time,
but he stopped changing the needle long ago,
putting on a conspirator's air,
for he feels keenly
that life too is piercing him
with one and the same spike,
when it long ago decided to cut him short
and not to bother about something that won't pull through ...

WALLS

It is a town and a night. But a night
that is afraid of dark houses
and of streets pulled down in the flanks of parks.
Another time so oncoming, it hesitates to advance,
another time so complete and with some extra for itself,
it looks around as if having lost something,
or as if there was something forgotten ...

And really, in this missed, indebted moment,
it steps nearer and does not yield itself fully until
a little window in the attic lights up
like postage due
on an obituary notice ...

SPRING TIME

Trees might have really blossomed again,
and again ten forces of flowers are here
for each week of the desert ...
The egg-like rhythm, full of passing-overs,
is maddeningly dimming out the senselessness of life,
while black seeds allow themselves to be deluded
by irritating light, which shivers
like a woman's chemise, when being dried
during the baking of funeral urns ...

Wheedling, auspicious, barely persuasive,
still without eyes, sightless and blind already,
we would gladly nurse at least our death
as a faithful sister of our nascence ...
And yet to each of us the earth is going to say one day:
I remember you, but I don't know why any more ...

AT THE END OF THE WORLD

It's here, in fact, the same as with a river
in the moment when it leaves an extinct lake:
a few haemorrhaged chasms, which don't know where they are,
a few pillars, coated with a marble semen of ideas
and a handful of old torn-up maps,
which are no match
for a bundle of banknotes of unknown origin
that irony, numb with cold, would find at the threshold
    of its door ...

From time to time, almost as a witness, an echo resounds,
like some kind of head-turning rustling ...
It's as if sorrow had passed through premonitions,
dressed in a white suit of no one ...

ENCOUNTER II

No, no, it is not I, my lady!
You are cheating your young self-blood.
Even in pleasure you would wait for a secret sign
of another sweat, the sweat that often lies down with a tear.
And you would want to plant
the moment of your thighs with another root,
when the tree of hate meets spittle ...

Could it be really I?
I see your being,
which shivers towards me
as if seeking
what of the future is contained in the trail of a night cloud
above a seemingly sleeping man ...

AT A FLEA MARKET IN PARIS

It was at the beginning of November. Day was forfeited
to the screeching fog. A crowd of black men,
hopelessly dressed in croaky shrouds,
dawdled from a rag-and-bone man's stall
to the stalls of old-clothes men,
and tried at each of them overcoats and cloaks,
and laid them aside again ... They did so
as being unbribable rather than as those
who can offer too little:
so noble was their poverty.

And they lived this way somehow at random:
from lousy warmth's memory into warmth's forgetting,
in the sarcastic space where nobody noticed them
their gestures like an orphan were shaking,
and their self-torturing laughter was relying
upon the music ear of death.

It was relying in vain ... For everything looked
as if every hour without monsters
was the enemy of eternity ...

A COUNTRYSIDE CALLED SULTRINESS

A recollection, drenched by the sweat of a danseuse
and distorted by the statue to salvarsan,
has slyly stirred in you the underground boom
of one of the nights ... And reading from the snake's motion
your now stubbornly lamenting, helpless loneliness
reveals to you a pervasive countryside,
where nothingness upon the rocks resembles a jump,
between whose thighs a fountain closes itself up
to the genitals of the dog days ...

AT THE VERY SOURCE

Cogitation in sleep's eye
has so much room for animal deities
that speech can more freely identify and lose itself in them,
like a poor child in its toy.
Its small hand with the candle of images,
titillated under its arm by a secret sign,
shivers through the grass on the grave of the first grave,
and on the grave of the last mortal.
And it is this small hand that at the brink of appearance
forces the tragedy of your whole being
to jump down into innocence ...

Ruins are still here ... What then, when they will be!

EN LA NOCHE SERENA

It is a night with a hole in the canvas of self-delusions,
under which an aging poet
bakes china, using cracked moon light.
Lonesome as he is, and worn out,
flustered by an ironic text under the notes of pulses,
he looks for a ray as abandoned as he is
and avoiding graveyards out of sympathy,
which dreads the living.

Not that he wouldn't exist ... But if he is before realisation,
he ceases to be if he has been realised ...

DEEP DOWN

Stars and words are not unrelated ...
But deep down, in front of the hereditary guilt of death,
there, where a female entrance into the underworld opens
    love,
desecrated by even a whisper,
it is the wings that serve the lover,
but it is the snake that serves the genii ...

IN A COAL SHOP

It's drizzling outside and people bring out flowers
    to the rain,
which defiles the hairy picture in the sand,
finger-painted there by a child.

However, here downstairs, it is a candle
that scoops things off brains,
founded on an encounter of a mole with a mole –
and it does it with the phantasm of thinking,
which, alive in its underground life,
is revealed after its extinction
as an unearthly death ...

Yet the night and its eternal future
at a more procreative obscuration of clay
irritate, with a fixed look, the same by the same:
suddenly they become a lived swallowing of the centres
    of a recollection,
of the midday recollection of a woman's milk,
jetted forth from the horror of a mute, rusty-red wrath
inside the narrowing eye of a rooster ...

KEATS

But yes, it is he! He who,
inside the poisoned walls of his consciousness,
sets on fire the prison yearbook of statues
and, at a revengefully inborn light, taught them to speak
words left out by the first day after the world's creation ...
Alas, he was allowed to do so only for a lustreless
and yet truly superfluous moment,
because to underground gods and dogs
juvenility is true only inside the child
who, mute and blind, died already in its mother ...

Space roars, with its chin in the palm of nothingness,
and it is in one place only where
the flattened deplored scent of an abandoned vermouth
and the gate to a slaughterhouse, bulged out like Homer's eye,
lurk ...

EVA I

I

In Eve's sleep, the dogs, let loose upon the night's blobber-
 lipped womb,
peel off their raving as far as the colour of a rose.
But she – how she trembles
and leans against the bleating niggardliness of the
 moments
that can't reach the feet of a man's foundation,
and against the moon, its reason protruding reekingly
 from its mouth!
And how she is shaken by the ensheathed
dependence of the Braille script of delight
on the bristled groping-around and the arisen proto-word
that dreads the forfeit of death!

II

But along her spine, there neighs
a boyish or mature flash of grass –
and she, ravishing, with her eyebrows painted
with a piece of charred rib
from the last eunuch,
with her breasts, which abandoned
the known mouths for unknown kisses,
and with her thighs, which are
on God's travels of tempting –
she nestles against you, shy, nostalgic,
artful, capricious and compassionate ...

But who would not ever feel her sex
like a merciless slit
into the main branch of the Tree of Knowledge?

COUP DE GRACE

Even what was supposed to take place long ago is
 happening now ...
But I saw at the fair of Gahatagat:
a grandmother, a pile of lacrimal bones
thrown into the habiliments of last hope,
had nothing on her board but a few
petty insect nymphs she was offering.
Looking at them with the sorrowful horror of a being
threatened by something that would happen before time,
she was shading them with an earnest little roof of her
 palms,
lest the sun warm them too much –
and when she might sometimes look up at the passers-by,
her hopeful look became madly insistent.

The passers-by, however, were truly only passing by.
And it was thus again only she who was
in a certain moment shaken by explosive motion of one
 nymph after another –
and as she stood there, intimately cognisant of the
 primeval wrong,
betrayed, but still somehow self-accused,
she didn't manage, even for all the others who were passing
 by, to pursue
the ardently sorrel departure of about twenty butterflies.

BLAKE

It was enough for him to appear ... And the concurrent
   presence
of syphilitic emptiness and of gold with the tongue,
grown into a monumental script,
ceased desecrating some cracks, fuzzy with anger
of weeping she-angels and water, bleating in an hourly
   hotel ...
The fall of the chopped-off penis of Uranus
(a fountainhead with a maypole of a graceful candytuft)
was swelling under a look at cultic holes;
it stiffened over ulcerous Windsor:
it blanched the night with the fairly blood-stained moon
to let it resemble to the chemise of the menstruating
   mother of gods;
it cracked like the lamp at the grave of Spartan Helena;
it loved, it cursed and it pleaded to the sex of poesy
for the pleasures of one hundred nights;
yes, for the pleasures of one hundred nights, of one
   hundred nights;
it pleaded and beseeched the sex of poesy,
and all that with the same sacred force with which a
   beloved thing
is cruelly seeking its own dumbness inside us,
its own dumbness and anxiety ...
But even in the anxiety is something terminal ... If you
   stayed alive,
then it is only because you, quickly, created a new one ...

CRUCIFIXION

All those who a few hours ago
were still sucking on plum pits to wet their spun work
were now descending into town
between a butcher's belly near an organ
and the town gasworks ... They made no noise and were in
 no hurry –
They were both gratified and disappointed like some town
 rabbits
fattened by a weeping willow.
They grew torpid, and their recent fat fury
found inside them less and less space
and was already callous like a woman's thighs in a man's
 coffin ...
Also their unusual stroll made them tired
because no tram was running today.
Some of them caught a bit of cold
and were sniffing at the rose-aspirin,
crushing peanuts
and proving to themselves, by that breakage of sound,
that it was a dry season – and soon all of them,
in the gradualness of their homes as in black priest's
 frocks,
changed the one-eyed picture for the blind brush of sleep ...

But it was the wife of Pontius Pilate
who came after midnight to the One up there
and tore the holey towel from his loins ...

WILL I BE FORGIVEN ONE DAY?

She came so unexpectedly from the smoking wicks of
 nocturnal streets!
And she was old and decrepit, decrepit almost indulgently,
with her face tipped over by a wilful hat
into the rushes of her wrinkles and bits and pieces of her
 smile,
with the hesitations of a child who
had the Host stuck to the palate,
and with a voice which didn't know any more
that everything belonged to it from poverty,
but which still didn't have enough.

She came so unexpectedly, and unexpectedly and
 wonderingly she said:
"Please, which way should I go, you know, please,
oh, which way should I go, yes, you know, which way,
well, it's not far, which way should I go, excuse me ..."
– but she could not remember, she was beating her
 forehead,
being set in motion by glowing, heavy pondering,
and always and again stopped close to her tears,
as a fire stops only when reaching the river ...

She came so unexpectedly ...
Will I be forgiven one day for abandoning her?

A VOICE AND A COUNTER-VOICE

I Then

It's night. At the bar, they are still pouring you the last one
with a discredit of compassion ... But behind you,
the body of some shockingly lonesome poor wretch,
falling in drunkenness from a butterfly to a caterpillar,
falling in despair between itself and itself,
from where there will be no escape for him,
reminds you, both untimely and slyly,
of two hillsides, shabby with rocks,
with well-preserved trees, with spluttered-up fornication in
    weasels' tails,
and with almost sky-blue consciousness of sparrow hawks.
Between the hillsides, a rivulet was running wild
like a fistful of snares thrown into the face of hearing.
You were young then ... You were taking no notice
how cruelly shabby was the handle to the graveyard ...
"Please, pour me one more!" ... Yes, and the sun
was coarse-grained like peacock's blood,
and you lay down, across that stream of water
from one bank to the other, boulder after boulder ...

After it grew dark, it was she who walked across ...

II And today

It's night. At the bar, they are still pouring you the last one
with a surly fatigue ... But let's not talk about it.
I don't know you, and everything is happening the same
    way
as when one comes across one another at the stairs:
one goes upstairs and the other downstairs ...
It is you who is down there now;
fortunately rum doesn't ask what happened to us both,
for it is still neither dust nor spittle,
and it's not raining into its grave.
Rum is good, though: you drink as the first one after me,
as the autumn drinks wine by oxen tears from chimneys
while inhaling the god of the moment ...
Of the moment? No, you know, permanently and fretfully,
inside out where the one who loved you lives.
Ah, desirably you know that, and magically you know that,
but you are here in such a lecherous desire and without any
    such transition
that the countryside too should have a collapsed bridge ...

YES, YOU KNOW –

Do you know that vinous gust
of a transnocturnal and transcendental whirlwind,
which suddenly turns numb
and peeks its eyes into the madmen's guard.
The word, unknown to the sentence written at a sweaty
 window,
got stuck in the land of Tongues;
incoherent music will now no longer yank
the penis from the adder's hole of senses;
the roofer's crosslet stopped its disruptive rocking;
vaulting of stones put itself to death
in the sleep of the ulterior sun;
the fountains stopped their "Lamartining";
children were killed between Ophelia's thighs,
and history lost the memory
of the toxic glands of its behaviour.

Torpor! Absolute torpor!
And torpor caused perhaps only
by the walk of a woodlouse
over the inside of doors
in a country loo,
or by a church mouse just finishing,
under a kneeling board,
its meal of human snot.

A DOG DAY AT CHLUMEC

Nothing, really nothing ... And a nothing put down for
 nothing,
which, so lavish of this circumstantial day,
remembers even its walled years of an old age
together with the illusory doors of escape! ...
The sun is ear piercing ... From its mouth to its anus,
from its belief about form to the cognition of its ruin,
a ghastly nun moth of the snake of Eden works its way,
having won so easily and thus, by the ease of victory,
was soon forced to creep back into itself ...

The grey in the fecund places of the world,
crumbling in appearances, and a bluish-grey wheeze
of all leaves to repudiate the tree,
and the straw tail of gods
cracking the whip into the dust of a graveyard! ...
A little more, a little bit more,
and the aridity would destroy even itself ...
In the backyard next door, however, they are bathing
 a dead man in a trough,
and a little stream of splashed-out water runs as far
 as to me ...

DURING THE CONSTRUCTION OF THE TOWER OF BABEL

You were there by way of punishment, namely as a hodman.
Our work, from morning face-pulling up to the fall
 of darkness,
was answering us as hardheartedly as a winter ground a grave
 digger,
and, already long ago, it cut the midriff out of our entrails,
and, already long ago, some feeling of hope for an escape was
 hardly more
than snot, stepped in by our bare foot.
The passing nature of all spiritual was so terrifying
that many of us would like to believe
in the immortality of our bodies.
We began encountering their doubles ...

As far as it concerns you ... But no! ...
It was enough that the wife of Psentostris
walked across the half-made asphalt embankment,
and that whole swelling inhuman construction in front of us,
which was supposed to become the survival of eternity,
suddenly appeared to you as a mere overreaching.

Ruins were so imminent
that they resembled the certainty of love ...

WHO ARE YOU?

I do not know if women are stilled called "my dove",
and I've never asked you whether you are happy.
You, miraculous, you do not care, and you enter my
    adoration
without my having to lie, be jealous, or deserve your love.
You, fruitful, you cuddle up to my sharp misery, giving
    yourself to it completely
without my feeling a wrongdoer.
You eat and drink with me all my hateful confusion,
which you have irradiated with your perceptible simplicity.
You moved me without my feeling better than I am,
as one can feel in one's fantasy,
composed for two hundred pianos.
You, free, you liberate me, and I cannot ask for more,
I cannot ask for more –
and yet, that agonizing anxiety in me,
the anxiety for someone whom I will never know!

To be alone is too much for one's double,
but, with you, it was always you whom I missed ...

ONE SINGLE PIECE OF HISTORY

I used to stand more than once (when one could drink God
and the devil could not be slept out);
I used to stand more than once at the little windows
    of night pharmacies
and lend my ear to all pleas, all sighs,
all questions and all thanks, to all heart openings,
and worries and anxieties, discoloured by frequent washing
    in tears
and by humiliation in front of shameless hope –
and I used to feel wafting through that wild-looking little
    window
both vexation and kindness and, other times, irritation
of an effervescent being in a white coat of never-ending
    waking up,
and the scent of miser's lilies, and also a surplus
of colourless poisons, which were handed out
only against the pawn tickets of possible recovery,
which, alas, in advance,
sold the eyes of all sickly men to emptiness –
and I used to see in that little window,
always, one hand watchful and the other drowsy,
one motherly and the other unconcerned,
but each of them trembling, and as if fried
in the oil from Solomon's lamp ...

And sometimes, a bent-down face appeared there,
which was spurning time so magnificently
that it looked like a hole in the wall of Paradise,
plugged up by the bottom of an angel ...

Then, later, as heavy as a pocket for the stones of
    maledictions,
all the more dolefully and fully in disfavour,
I used to be on the point of a desire to hear
the voice of the first-born rooster,
and, soon afterwards, the forenoon creeping up
when the shouting of playing children
restrains sadness as red flies do at a funeral ...

DEATH

You drove him out of your heart many years ago,
and you locked that nook and tried to forget everything.
You knew that he was not in music, and so you were
    singing;
you knew that he was not in silence, and so you stood mute;
you knew that he was not in loneliness, and so you stayed
    alone ...
Yet, alas! what has happened today,
when you were horrified like someone
who, suddenly, in the middle of the night, saw
a ray of light under the door
leading to the next sitting room,
where, long since, nobody lives any more?

IT IS TODAY ...

It is today a little lake deep inside you,
which just recently dried up,
but how quickly it fills up with tears.
It is today an airfield deep inside you,
just recently abandoned,
but how quickly it is grown over with grass.
So, with your headwaters of grief, you should go on foot ...
But you stay frozen
because you see, closely in front of you,
cockroaches, moving across the lane
from the butcher's to the baker's ...

LIFE I

Aside from a profane rutting place,
there stands a morgue,
easily expandable, timeless almost. Its building,
some limestone pounded together and a little turret,
has never pressed upon you to begin with a thought about
    extinction,
and end with a cypress ... No, if it horrified,
then it was only by its decrepit state,
even if they were still interring many here ...
However, all those years of yours,
you passed along a hundred times and a hundred times
    it was the same,
so you grew so accustomed to it that you didn't see it.

But today, its one and only window has revealed
sweet curtains, printed here and there with flowers ...

WHAT WE HAVE SEEN ON THE FIRST DAY AFTER THE EXPULSION FROM THE GARDEN OF EDEN

It was a little piece of land, an impatient land but already
    tired of waiting,
a solemn little piece of land ... In its novelty,
there was not the least indication of punishment, not even
    of a change of place.
It was a jug full of wine,
not drunk up under Yggdrasil yesterday,
which we found today on a small herbivorous boulder,
from where a lovely plum tree lane ran.
We refreshed ourselves and heard somewhat exaggeratedly:
behind us bliss that we forced into evanescence,
and in front of us everything
that the sultry languor keeps permanent in mystery ...

It is true that dusk fell down a little earlier here
than we might have become used to,
and not until today do I understand why a nightingale's eye
was syphilitic, like the dial
on a personal weight scale in the city park ...
It is also true that I didn't eventually rely upon chaos
in that brash nightfall,
but what surprised me was Eve,
who crawled behind me,
somewhat both knowing and culpable,
and trampled something into dust ...
How could I have thought of
the golden section of music, lunulated for the first time?!

ALL THE TIME THE SAME

I know a being who buys
veils from the brides whose weddings came to nothing.
And I know a being who delays a wedding
because lovers could not afford engagement rings.
But that being, crammed into a chenille petticoat
of venerable and thus an already immortalized addiction,
is not as heartless as she may appear!
She knows how to approach all deceived and abandoned
    maidens,
and exactly in that moment when even loneliness
    renounces them;
she knows how to exchange the love that passes away
for the compassion that's not happening;
and she knows how to whisper to them boldly:
"I will keep my hand at your belly,
and wait until I feel a kick in it ..."

THE SIRENS DIED AWAY

Today, at night and in my dreams, I told myself:
"Bitter is thirst, and somehow distraught that it drinks
    from fate
like a rag marionette thrown by a child into its pisspot.
Bitter is passion, because it has everything
in such a pressing nearness that even mystery is out
    of reach.
Bitter is art, and in such a black colour that it would come
    off
only with the sweat of a female armpit, if death was
    a woman.
Bitter is consciousness that catches itself on things
like a blunt razor that was used to shave a dead man.
Bitter is all this – and yet it would be good
to awake and keep a vigil!"

It was, however, the four-times-stubborn angels of a hearse
who carried me away to the quietus;
it was the angels whom I heard
whispering one to another endlessly:
"Don't wake him up, be quiet, quiet, don't wake him up!"

SIGNS

Art began with the fall of angels ...
The time of chaff, of heaps of dung, of squelched Sweet
    Flag,
of unburnt ashes and of tongues ruined by cream,
the time shaving its hair off the thighs of a prostitute:
it seems only to vilify.

But the time of pebbles, of a stepmother's combing and
    a dog's limping,
the time of coughing in cellar dwellings,
the time of the grave digger who seems to want
dig through the earth into a more genuine life,
the time of cervical vertebrae during a jump
over a midsummer night's fire,
the time that does not need our help at all:
it still does not have enough weight.

Art began with the fall of angels.
But they too drank wine, broke bread for themselves,
and slept with mortal women –
and so, bedazzled, we pretend again, looking for the signs
on the table slashed by the knife of Orpheus ...

CLEOPATRA

Music, with knees clutched together by the beer of ancient
    Egypt,
sits inside a statue ... As the statue rises, music lies down.
As the statue reclines, music kneels down.
As the statue extends, music saturates.

This is repeated a hundredfold,
as long as the baptismal force of the spine
won't subvert the pillar of the wet vault.

What to do then with what's unembodied in time?
And yet, exactly this became for us a passion
which regards woman as eternity ...

A LINE

The line of virginity, the line of love,
mystery, cleaved asunder by the fall of Adam's brainy star;
and fate, which throws there, using eagles' eggs,
death, quelled by a child's cry in a valley ...

The concurrent presence of roaring nightingales
and meteors, destroying the city,
is only the consequence of an angel's feelings in a brothel,
is only the consequence of God's thoughts as a bricklayer ...

POESY

If man does not feel lost,
lost is he to everything that is happening in the others
and is going to happen in him.
And lost to all that, he writes a letter and an envelope,
and he seals and underscores Do not open until my death!

However, to be lost and to endure,
and to have the moon already in his book
but the night only in his reading,
to know neither the end nor the edge of himself,
not to be alone but to be lost,
that's as if one's own and some strange pain
had borne a third heart ...

A ROOSTER IS SINGING

Mundane, crude cultic pits,
and yet the Holy Ghost
was embedding its hair roots exactly into these ...

The opening and looting of mounds,
and yet a hermit's vein
was swelling exactly into these ...

Desire permeates the most conscious reality,
but that what is jealously cast back is a mystery,
threatening us by the demise of divinity,
if we won't start again ...

WE ARE MISTAKEN

Why say that joys of the mortals are nothing more
than lightning bolts upon goose feathers?
I remember certain moments of my childhood
when a bill sticker stood near a barn,
his bicycle leaning at a plum tree ...
One week later, a circus arrived.
It was such an erupting crowd-puller
that one had to bring in more chairs.
Never, never ever shall I see again such miracles.
Acrobats pulled down the roller blinds of their T-shirts;
an equestrienne waited for a secret sign of my love;
a harlequin was stitching up our brains with a froggy floss
and Easter week's threads of illusions;
and a rope walker burnt his movements with candles for
    so long
that, until I, together with all lakes,
turned everything inside me upside down ...
But most of all I enjoyed sawdust,
from which a cloudlet of beginning
took every lightning of fulfilment.
But alas, how quickly that joy turned cold,
when I came to know
that sawdust was delivered to the circus
by the largest coffin works of the nearby town!

THE EYES

The eyes of the mortals, the miraculous eyes!
The eyes of a man, the eyes of a girl,
miraculous eyes, really miraculous!
His eyes, the eyes of desire! Her eyes, the eyes
    of temptation!
His eyes, blindly descending into two fruit stones
to shoot forth into a tree ...
Her eyes, heavy like the flake of virginity
but feather light, like the bloom of that tree
and the fruit of that tree!

A LANDSCAPE

The feeling of a lake, in danger that it will be betrayed
by the flight of thirteen hundred swans,
steps out on the firm land, keeps watch for a while,
then strays and stops under a sour cherry tree
in order to look in forgetful wonder at the ground
where heaps of fruit stones had already turned white.

A child, who spat out these stones here a while ago here,
wades, at this moment, through the rushes
and, at the end, frightens thirteen hundred swans ...
He looks at them full of wearisome happiness,
lies down on the eroded crumbling shore
and falls asleep there, curious about where he may wake up ...

A WALL

A beautiful limy wall, which is mirrored in dung water,
receives from eternity more than the stone upon a crypt.
Without conclusion, without cognition and still warmly,
it lives between God and men,
and its sole distended crack
is looked upon, from God's side, by a horse,
and, from the men's side, by a protruding drawbar.

A beautiful and cruel wall!

AT A VILLAGE GRAVEYARD AT THE WALL OF SELF-MURDERERS

Here, where sneezeweed kisses the photograph of the
 diseased,
and where the nun of a tombstone has the stained
 movement of marble
within the cackle of geese ... oh yes, exactly here
everything assents as well that man was not created
but made. Things also were only made.
Man and things, made for the reproof of the dead.
Things wait. Man forebodes.
Things beseech. He resists.
Things grow old and linger on. He is immortal and dies
 away.
Things are forsaken and he is lonesome,
and he is not lonesome only then,
when his life is turning against itself ...

ENCOUNTER III

High in the mountains, in the midst of self-sown boulders
and an uncropped waterfall, I met an old man.
He said to me (cheerfully, but in such a way
that his seclusion wouldn't know about it):
"You are the only one who has found me here;
surely, you must have died many years ago!"
Why, I asked, and he answered:
"Earlier I used to leave behind me my hideout made
 of branches,
my fireplace, a little bit of tobacco and food, or a sign.
But as I ascended higher and higher,
I was convinced that no one would follow me any more,
so I cut it out ... When did you die?"
I hardly remember, I answered, woebegone.
And he added: "How could it be! ... But
you have in yourself still a little of the sun from the god
 Quetzalcoatl ...
Switch it off so that you see all that is illuminated by the
 moon!"

EODEM ANNO PONS RUPTUS EST

Joy!
It is joy; it really is; it is indeed!
And he felt it, and not like something merciless
that comes dashing along with such a ferocity
that it extinguishes in us our unprotected fire,
or like something vertiginous that, at the double light of
    irony,
brings to us a bottle and shoes set for dancing –
oh no, what he felt was silent, simple, unfounded joy,
not the one entrusted only for a while, but a donated joy,
the joy of a man who just walks across a bridge
and will sing from now all the time ...
But it was enough for a dead leaf
brought down by the wind to him –
and the bridge was overloaded ...

A WALL

A wall ... A wall so spiritual that it can now only vilify,
a wall that deprives a tempted soul of any motion
and the motion of nostalgia for gashes into the miraculous,
yet a wall somehow humiliated by the mystery
of why it stays here – and balancing this feeling
by being so tall and not crumbling ...

THE DEATH OF A POET

His last desire was not complicated:
it was a child, craving a letter from a chimney sweeper.
His last gesture was quite simple:
he threw away hospital bed sheet,
into which a picture of a straddled woman was woven in.
His last nakedness was quite simple:
no one was kissing it,
not even alms vouchers were issued for it.
His last eyes were quite simple:
they kept silent with such a confession that no one dared to say
that everything was worm eaten this year.
And his last recollection was the recollection
of a foggy September morning,
a long time ago and somewhere long ago beheld,
the recollection of a sour cherry twig,
reddish, permanent, even *faithful*,
which popped up from the fog, ending nothing ...

ETERNITY

Do you want to anticipate eternity? Aren't you scared?
If you are really not scared, and if you don't rely
upon the testicles of roosters –
walk along the streets in which the acacia is fading,
and a cranefly, and a baking tin,
and then set out around the tobacconist's and around milk
    cans
at about three o'clock in the morning,
exactly at the moment when the last kingpin
and strumpet have rustled across,
at the moment when nobody yet knows
whether cigarettes, buns and milk
are for the dead or for the living ...
But you must wear canvas shoes on your feet ...

A SUITCASE

It is an old man who hasn't been able,
now for two years, to get into his suitcase because he lost
    the key
and because he is afraid to ask his daughter for some
    money to call a locksmith.
In that suitcase, he keeps a few trinkets
that could still warm his heart a bit:
some photos from his youth, when he was soldiering in
    Bosnia,
a handful of letters, rather faded and doubtful,
to let him dream over them,
his submachine gun, and a dickey for a ball
signed once for him by Cléo de Mérode.
But, in particular, he has there a sizable hook
and a rope, stronger than the hair of seven angels ...

Oh, the old man knows well that one doesn't need a rope
    and a hook,
and that one can simply jump from the window ...
But he does not know that this is exactly what his
    neighbour
from the house opposite has been waiting for all this time,
a neighbour who is painting his hair with an ink-pencil,
and who attends only the funerals of self-murderers ...

HAVE A LOOK

Have a look at that beautiful old furniture,
so very and so soothingly beautiful
that it is somehow saved
by a miserable iron folding bed in the corner!
The furniture was made by a mute joiner
who was making it for the sake of centuries,
but the bed wobbles, gathers rust and talks about
how finite love in despair wants to renovate eternity,
although it hasn't ceased to be ephemeral ...

A CANVAS
To Josef Šíma

A coarse hemp canvas, a beautiful canvas,
excitingly fitting the body of a woman
who stands between God and men ...
A painter longs to cover it with his retreating humbleness,
a sculptor would be glad to enclose it into an even more
    chaste form,
and a poet, standing in front of it, knows
that we don't see what's not concealed.
But a woman will provocatively rip it open
between God and man ...

A STATUETTE

That clay slate statuette, which stayed for so long,
unjustly and shamefully,
in the window of a shop
where only hard sweets are sold,
is now with me ...
Leaning with its heel against an astronomical atlas
and illuminated by the time to come, it throws its shadow
    backwards
on the firewall of poesy.
Because it lives with a mortal, it is somehow a witness
to his vices, sins, remorse and despair,
but because it is going to outlive him, it is also his hope
that once, in a rightful summary, it will tell who he was.
And it knows how to talk ... Just yesterday it told me:
"There are the poor who despise the poor.
How come you have recognized me?
There is no one any more who recognizes me! ..."

PEOPLE

People are so explicit in their selfishness that it makes one shudder
and so diffused by their routine
that they are invisible to each other.
As it concerns the former, I recall a teacher
who, after local manoeuvres, used to take children to a meadow;
nothing but horse dung was there, but he emphasized:
"don't miss noticing how aligned the droppings are!" ...
And the latter? Ask the builders of cities
why the apparently living can barely tolerate
those really dead,
and that only in apartment houses ...

GODS ARE ...

Gods, with beautiful straw pigtails,
with easily susceptible tinder of spirituality,
and with cloaks buttoned with dry peas,
are forbidden to warm themselves at our kitchen fire,
at glassworks, or at flagellating fornication ...
Out of carefulness and fear of humiliation,
they don't even know the sun, and only the lunar solstice
is allowed to tempt them and lure them
closer to the bliss of mortals,
but under the condition that they never step out
of eternity, so needful to them ...
Marvel at them, then, that when Eve once burned Adam's manuscript
(a poem about the mark on their wedding bed sheet),
they began to envy both the pot of soup
which started out boiling under the paper
and the cruel flame which is destroying us
between our knees and our elbows ...

AN AUTUMNAL NIGHT AT A LAKE

No, not even music, just keep quiet!
Darkness can indeed be inside a chock-full clock,
when the park swells up with the cramps of a statue,
but the night is exactly only one moment, this moment,
when a sun's ray slaps the mud,
helping a water thief catch an eel with a fork
and, with the heavy spittle of a close-lipped man,
it hisses over a falling star,
the pittance a mosquito's yawn will drink away ...

NOTHINGNESS

Nothingness, omnipresent and so very common
that it could often manifest itself,
yet nothingness that is modest, a self-denying nothingness ...
And still everyone is afraid of it, no one wants it,
and so, brought to death by no one,
it thrives somehow, and its definiteness grows
as does the number of your empty bottles in the garret,
those bottles that you used to offer, but nobody cared for
    them,
and so you will take them out at night
and secretly pile them up in the street ...

Someone shouts there: "Knowing, you will not know!"
And someone else: "Woe to them, the fat dogs!"

THE TURK'S FIELD

An ancient trunk of a pear tree, lacerated by lightning,
appears here as beautiful as a dotted column in
    a storehouse.
And the boulder in fog reminds me of a pythoness,
who steams her bottom with boiled violets.
"All piles up, all rises up!" say both fruit and corn.
"All is underneath!" say sex and death.
And those who hoe the earth here are finding bones
and, from a small handheld quern-stone
and from coins discovered near them,
they figure out that the bones belonged to man ...

ALL THE TIME AGAIN

All the time that absence – more, that desolateness,
a desolateness with all the signs of cruelty
and held in custody, this most independent one
of never expressed qualms ...

Powerless of any defiance, you don't even defend yourself,
and yet, one can't otherwise, O you, the already
    commenced tear!
What we deserted holds us,
and that which deserted us gave us itself!

A DANSEUSE

You are the only reality that can change names
without renouncing conception and kin ...
And this might have been the only reason
why I never could compare you secretively
with a picture, a flower, a flame or the wind.
And this might have been the only reason
why I always felt sorry
for those beautiful, patient bare feet,
soiled by the dust of boards.
And this might have been the only reason
why you are for me humanly temporal, and thus your
    breath pants
from your belly to your breasts, which are superstitious
like two storms on a midsummer night.
You work without lakes ... But music roars and wants
    a drink
and prowls through the seductive dusk of movements
at least up to your sweat,
while I, who am not allowed to lie, can undeservedly see
that all the spots for kissing are exactly only on you.
But you throw them away beyond retrieving
for you need nothing more, not even yourself ...

AT A CEMETERY

When, outside, petty life strives and aspires,
and when, just behind the wall, a child carries some
 sausages from the market
and sits down in the bushes and smells them covetously
but mustn't eat even a single one
because they are counted –
here, as the story goes, all is asleep ...
It is, however, only an imposed sleep,
and the stones here are like the dentures
that people take out before narcosis,
telling their dear in the waiting room:
"No need to stay here, I am going to scream!"
But they don't scream, and despite our liking to stay with
 them,
there is always someone who leads us, sobbing, away,
leads us away into life, which struggles and strives,
except that it's into a life whose gifts
repel us more and more,
because they have been counted ...

AT A WAYSIDE CROSS

There are moments which see only themselves,
and only because they are not conscious.
A voice would express them only then
if the moon came out from your word into the mouth of the
 dead.
And every certainty harms them so much
that they entice you into a foggy countryside,
where you catch sight of nothing more than a wayside
 cross,
yes, nothing more than a wayside cross ...
Does it want to help you, if it appears to you,
as if Jesus were on the cross and Christ at the crossroads? ...

WHEN I BREATHED IN THE SCENT

It's not long ago when I met in the street
an unknown girl. She was returning from the Corpus
    Christi Feast
and wore a bridal wreath atop her head. I admired it
and praised it and spared no spontaneous words,
and I still hadn't finished when she said:
"Whatever, but how sweetly it smells!"
And when I breathed the scent in, at once I understood
that because of a certain scent we must soon die
without having completed lauding those things
that radiate from it ...

AN ENCOUNTER IV

No, this one had never eaten up a pie
into which a girl mixed a drop of her menstrual blood.
No, this one had never waited for his bride,
who was dressing herself in the kneading trough.
No, this one had never become entangled in a wedding robe:
he had a face which he, here and there, washed
in an old stony coffin
and dried it with a horse mane. His slashed-up face.
He had eyes that could see only
a prophesy to be fulfilled,
and he was using both hands as the right hand of blessing ...
His legs were all the time knocking down
the frontier posts of a forbidden gesture,
and all his appearances were suggesting to you
that he had lived for a long time under a false name
and would now say: In fact, I am ...
But he did not say that, and he was not even here. He just
    lingered here.

AN ENCOUNTER V

Stopped by a woman in the gate of an unknown town,
I pleaded with her: "Let me in; I will only enter
and step out again and enter again only for stepping back,
because I am as afraid of darkness as every man is."
But she said to me:
" Look, I left the light burning there!".

THEY ARE IN A HURRY

They have no time for themselves; they are afraid to be
> alone;
but they niggardly gobble history, the dead, reality, even
> paintings;
they drink all that down with the two-colour urine of
> goddesses,
who keep their menstrual cycle in travel books;
they are in a hurry to swallow side-faced apparitions
> without the gift of revelation
and thus bury themselves with a mortifying consistency
> under masks;
they never have enough of property, landmarks and habits
to explain everything with a voracious eagerness,
and, when their funeral bell tolls,
they are congested with their fate,
while God may be a spectator of voids
not destined to be fulfilled ...

SHE ASKED YOU

A young woman asked you: What is poetry?
You wanted to say to her: It's also that you are, ah yes, that
    you are,
and that in fear and wonder
which bear witness to a miracle,
I am dolefully jealous of your beauty's ripeness,
and because I can't kiss you or sleep with you,
and because I have nothing, and whoever has nothing to give
must sing ...

But you didn't say that to her; you remained silent,
and she didn't hear your song ...

SHROVE TUESDAY

In the decrepit plaster of the town, shaken by the song
 of nothingness
like a decoration on an opera stage,
in a disreputable habit of pedestrians
walking blindfolded outside themselves,
in the movement of fingers which imitate centipedes
as centipedes imitate the spine of sardines,
in walls turning cloudy,
in which there are more windows than children,
and in the air, which likes the blue colour,
he chooses grey, and black is the result.
Yes, in everything that can't multiply fate into simple love
by insults, anxiety and impoverished suffering:
a single sunray appears,
illuminating a baby pram,
which could not fit into the tram any more ...
And at the same time someone asks Galileo: "Is the sun
 eternal?"
And he answers: 'Eternal? No! But very old!'

A VISION

How dumbfounded you were! You went down the pit
with a miner's lamp of despair
and stopped at a beer joint ...
And exactly then he appeared to you ...
Why are you worried, he said cheerfully;
it is quite simple:
He who comes to see God and has already renounced all
    that is mundane
will find anti-earth at the end.
And he who is returning from God, rich again with
    everything,
meets, once more, man ...

WITH THE LEAST ATTACHMENT

He came to me just when we were arriving
at the last tram stop ...
Pointing under the seats,
he said with a smile: "Look,
someone has forgotten one galosh here! ..."
I could really see its hollow measure and visualize
a drenched foot, splashing just now through slush
    somewhere,
but he added with a joyful voice:
"Man is so immodest that he lives between himself and
    himself
and, at the same time, complains about a chasm,
even building two tombs for himself:
one for his body and the other for his name
solely to save himself for the memory of his grandchildren,
and, only sometimes and almost unwittingly,
there remains after him something dispensable,
    godforsaken;
but it's exactly this godforsaken staff that relieves
his other, contemporary journey, the journey to eternity ..."

PASSING BY

When life, a long-ago extinct life,
begins to winnow oats for its dead horses in a distant
    desert
and then makes a sortie with them here, to us –
a living being is about to take into his trembling hands
a brick from the Ashurbanipal's library
and, contemplating that act, quits the present ...
After a short while, they meet each other somewhere in
    space,
but, without stopping, each one flies farther somewhere
    else
in order not to recognise the other ...

THE PASSION WEEK

Could it really be that I am alone again?
Could it be that I love too little
and am seldom silent, and don't suffer enough
and consider freedom
as my never being completely in my fate?

Could it truly be that I don't understand that man gives
    only
when nothing has been left for him?
Could it truly be that I am full of those proud colours
that irritate the light of nothingness so as to be pulled out?

Art too, when the heart serves the pulses
like a typesetter's little lamp,
left me for my double
and makes light of me somewhere, creating now all the
    more,
the more I deserve to be trampled over
in my flagellated aridity.

It rains only outdoors. Truly the right season
for the wolf to come and catch swans
while the roar of rafted timber is to be heard this far –
by its wet persecution mania –
the timber to make coffins for all existing ...

ENCOUNTER VI

It was greasy papers that began to terrify him in his dreams.
Then he was refusing to eat
and ordered all pictures to be taken off the walls.
And one day, he, always so careful with his keys,
left everything open and went away,
and he didn't even take his coat, though it was freezing,
and it was January, that month when strange dogs
start appearing in the suburbs, abandoned by their lords
who don't want to pay for dog tags ...

One heard that a hammer slipped away
from a roofer's hand and killed the old man.
Soon after his death, I met him on the stairs to Letna park.
He was begging, but accepting the alms only from those
who were descending, so that they had it somewhat lighter ...

THIS TOO

This too is your lot: to witness bitterly lewd silence,
and just at those moments when only the Underworld
 knows
what a woman dares before a man decides,
both right in the middle between a fallen tree of youth and
 an excrement of an old age.
This too is your lot:
to witness bitterly the adulterous lechery of music,
and this exactly at those moments when, she, pushed into
 her crotch,
thrusts forth her breasts
so as to sough then from her nefarious mouth to you
through the wall, cracked by Agamemnon's fall ...

THE SMILES

Many are the smiles.
But I think about the one most difficult for us:
the plainest smile.
It is a tormenting smile, furrowed up criss-cross
by the vintner's knife of time;
the smile that needs just one more wrinkle
to unravel everything and be ready for the whole name
    of God.
Such a smile remains on the face
a little longer than the joy from which it emerged –
or it is the smile that senses joy and precedes it,
so as to disappear at its presence
and leave the whole face only to it ...

IN THE VERY MORNING

A dripless candle and its deep rooted flame are enough
for darkness to catch jaundice, for the curtain, inflated into
    the street,
the stye of a star, and for time to have those distances
that, like the distances upon a statue,
you can measure only by the fear from people ...
It is surely the right moment, when a sick man thumbs
the diamond edition of fixed ideas,
and when the dead come from him into him,
those talking dead, who suddenly, during their talk,
remember the music and set about to play dumb.
What music this can be, if it evokes the dawn,
the departure of bliss, and a hard lining-up
of all the opposite lightning rods,
which the alive place exactly above lavatories?

LOVERS I

Innumerable eyes of elderberries, thrown into the sun,
the seminal blindness of man, spurted into darkness,
the darkness by which he alone
reveals to himself first his very self
and then her: a mere girl,
who, suddenly knowing, lies alarmed here
with her mons of burnt music, with grass on her grave ...

REMBRANDT

Rembrandt perceived it ... And he knew
that a chipped wall, a cracked grape, a woman-woman,
who are not here as an abyss,
cannot be a sign.

Rembrandt knew it ... And he felt about
what decided that the most plain dish
served on the most expensive plate
is repeated in the vicinity of an ideal
upon the lustre of a mortuary fly.

Rembrandt perceived it ... And he knew
that souls are between themselves and their selves,
so that they might not escape from themselves,
but that a genius is an unceasing presence ...

AT A FUNERAL

Old and abandoned ... Really abandoned?
She needed very little ... Once in her youth,
she walked with a man ... The odour of his armpit was so
	pungent
that it was splitting her open as far as the awareness of her
	womb ...
Ashamed and confused by his cajolery,
she plucked a leaf of hawthorn along the way
and lived off it all her life ...

A GRAMOPHONE RECORD

"That record is broken!" says a demonic voice ...
And truly, a black-golden ray of nothingness
gets stuck in the crack between God and men,
a prickle of insecurity scrapes at the crack in a graveyard wall,
and the sting of mystery scratches the crack in a woman.

We play ... We play catch with time,
but everything goes on turning ... From there our
consciousness, the consciousness of mere appearances ...

ENCOUNTER VII

It was in the streets of Athens, where space
had cut itself by some tetrachordal music
and turned speckled upon the ermine of cubism.
A little farther, a watchman of statues was marking
    his time.
"The statues?" he said. "It's children who mostly come
    to see them,
silent children ... But the silence of children
will not change if we, the adults, would also keep silent;
no, it lasts usually just a little longer ...
Such a lengthiness only poets may still understand,
surmising that there are only as many words
as there is time contained in a vision ..."

A HUMAN VOICE

A stone and a star don't compel us into their music;
flowers are silent; things almost conceal something;
a beast denies, because of us, inside itself
the harmony of innocence and mystery;
the wind always contains the chastity of a mere sign,
and what singing is, only muted birds know,
those to whom you tossed an unthreshed sheaf on
    Christmas Eve.

To them it's enough to be, and this can't be voiced. But we,
we are afraid, and not only in the dark,
and we don't see our fellow man
even in a fruitful light,
and, panicking into a furious exorcism,
we shout: "Are you here? *Speak!*"

AN EVENING CLOUD

Unconscious by its transition and juvenile by time's
 unconsciousness,
it returns play's verbal testament to silence ...
But its trustfulness into an immobile motion
might have been shorter
if wild geese, prepared to fly away,
had not just appeared under it ...
Then it becomes fixed even more musically
and is already illusory, because it is amorous ...

And you, an unworthy witness of its bliss,
hardly dare to ask about
what has decided that anxiety hasn't yet attacked the heart
when it was so defenceless ...

AN ABYSS OF AN ABYSS

Love towards God destroys itself
so that God has space.
Love towards oneself and one's neighbours
destroys both the destroyer and the neighbours
so that God has time.
But we do not love God, thus destroying love
so that nothingness has space.
But we love neither ourselves nor our neighbours, thus
 destroying God
so that nothingness has time ...

IN THE KITCHEN

You have not been here for almost one year ... You were
 afraid to enter ...
And just having done so, the emptiness, once imploring
and then spurned, lost all love for you now,
wilfully beseeching you to pay
for your presence by your presence ...
Everything here is finding fault with you:
linoleum, some kindling wood, a scorched fly,
bread mould, embittered vinegar of cracks
and oxalic stains and the tan of pulled-down air
and cobwebs, spluttering from the lookouts of nooks
and quite underneath is silence, exactly at the spot
where the moon shines only during the day ...
Among all these things, however, you suddenly notice
(with a cruel, most ordinary and thus the most mysterious
and seemingly lifelong certainty)
a coffee cup and traces of some make-up on it,
where once the lips of the one who deserted you
pressed themselves for the last time ...

TWO OF THEM

Two stars on the forehead of a sky-born cow
pull themselves down into themselves by their overripe
    heaviness
so that later, when falling, they could mingle
Apollo's parabola with the nape of a drunkard
and steer into the diamond shire of Mallarmé ...

Even if we overtake consciousness, we screen ourselves by
    inspiration.
And so, in the intimate rays of the two stars' light,
one can glimpse only the wall of a seedy gooseberry bush,
where two women chuckle without knowing why,
when, squatting, they look at each other and urinate ...

ENCOUNTER VII

It was a miraculous little boy,
if a miracle is what we still don't understand
but already love ... He was in his sixth year
and was teasing the healthy eternity ... It's less than one week
since he died from diphtheria ... I didn't go to his funeral ...
But today I have met him at the cinema ticket counter ...
He said to me in confidence:
"I saw the movie already – one month ago,
but I have to see it once more
because I don't know whether the princess, who is acting in it,
left the balcony or not ...

CONSTRUCTIONS FOR ETERNITY

There are constructions for eternity, noble constructions,
from which, at the end, remained and survived
only a bloated, whitewash-stained bucket,
which, full of snakes' scuts,
splits its sides laughing, being tickled by fame ...

The echo of this lets one surmise
that the constructions were tall, and that only a legless house painter
was allowed to embellish their interiors ...

You went through them all: youth and passion and vainglory,
which used to quench torches
by one hit of a fist and a spit at a candle –
now they sell here, like an incendiary, just soot
or some udder-like dust,
vaulted up under a falling cowpat,
as the only bronze for the acidic wrinkles of gods
or hired murderers ...

WHEN A BOY

When a boy looks for obscene words in a dictionary,
and he would want more, and they are not there
(because the blobber-lipped woman became disreputable
and the gold-bearded man was struck mute), he begins
    fabricating them ...
Soon, however, being tempted by a mere,
even if a sad-blooded, premonition,
which, locked and bolted, lost all love for knowledge,
he feels wronged, his whole consciously wishful light
reflecting itself, again and again, from all counterparts into
    his heart,
the same way the sun must return into itself with all the
    rays
it emitted onto a barber's signboard ...
At the end, his cruel purity is so unembodied
that, in front of any woman,
he can do nothing more than hate ...

SHE I

I hear a man who panic-stricken, asks:
"O joy, was it so bad for you with me
that you stayed no longer than a little while?
Mightn't I have loved? Was I too tight for you?
Did the swelter of nocturnal deities stand in your way?
And didn't you have enough silence,
because exactly at that moment a silversmith was arguing
in me with a goldsmith about a diamond of reason?"

And I hear how joy is answering him:
"No, no, but I am *irrepressible*!"

EVERYTHING

The night, drunk away by black-and-gold poesy,
love, permitting evil,
bliss and its knowledge of poisons ...
Everything was stunned, lived; everything loved.
Everything was in one breath, in one move and embrace.
Everything died too in one common death,
but was then quartered and thrown down
into different graves ...

LOVERS II

A long time ago, the god of laughter and song
had already closed Eternity behind himself.
Since those times, it is only rarely
that a diminishing recollection resounds in us.
Since those times, it is only pain
that never comes life-sized
but is always greater than man.
And yet, it must fit into his heart...

LIKE IN A FILM ...

Like in a film ... semen is jetting out
on the wedding-bed sheet of image and leakage.
Cleopatra, with rings on her feet
and diamonds in the dint of her belly button,
illuminates those aroused instinctive gestures,
which we are later so ashamed of –
and Onan is doing what he can to let them feel more roomy ...
Yet only time, shivering between a pillar and a rift,
knows well that when love consents to evil,
evil rejects evil because it rejects love ...

THEY TOLD HIM

They told him: "The devil is about to leave this earth.
Go and find out what people think about it!"
However, a typed report of a scientist
could make reference only to apathy ...

They told him: "A second Adam is about to come.
Go and find out whether the second paradise is here!"
However, the testimony of a graveyard surveyor
could make reference only to a wasteland ...

IN THE PROVINCE

Your eye, etched by the last buttercup,
twinkles with blissful but already impatient pain
and throws, then, in front of itself the first stage of the
 evening.
The sunset is plain. There is nothing in it
that could baffle a potato road,
leading straight into a village,
above which smoke rises up
with a promise that supper is being prepared ...
A few figures stand under a walnut tree
which catches the motion of their hands
as they talk about black horses with loose shoes.
A few rapid sounds, softly bitter
like a piece of lint on thighs,
open themselves into warm walls ...
And that's all ... And yet, who could deny
that it does not concern buildings, but cottages,
and thus not houses, but his home? ...

IT RAINED

Pockmarks after the smallpox of rain ...
Small hollows scooped out by a fingernail into the bruised
 fruit.
Birdweed, losing colour like wombs.
Holes in the sails of a ship without wind.
Deck openings into which no mast will be sunk.
Theatre on the day when there is no play.
Seeds without wings, uterus without cognition.
Self-born echoes without an orphan's song.
Even tombs are empty ...

A VILLAGE NOON

A drummer on a village green ... Each of his beats
reminds you of all those little balloons
that flew away from the world of children into the world of
 animals.
Exiled from both, you feel spellbound
about how hair, canvas and glue
can hold the blind man's holiday with a scull ...

SO

This is that special moment: A boy spits on his handkerchief
and nurses a little girl's soreness.
A youth moves away to a pillar
and returns from the puberulent waist of ruins,
after he spilled everything that was upright.
A girl stays fully in half-eyed apertures,
and her finger can see the one she loves.
Men are horrified by the movement of Christ's wounds
on the body of the stigmatized.
Women comb their hair. And when women comb their hair,
they think about death and are scared to look into a mirror ...

WHEN

When man is alone, he longs for hiding even more,
so that nobody would see him.
Because uncertainty is frosty, agitated and communal
like a drunkard in a church door.
Because certainty is soothing, and unadorned like a grave,
and the grave like the place
from which, in the spring, snow begins to disappear first ...

PER PROCURAM

Not until they are evicted from their home can they
 comprehend
that the sitting room is theirs. But they don't persevere,
and, hardly surmising that the red that their eyes have
 inherited from tears
can't be the measure of dry things,
they immediately appeal to the law for sympathy.
Yet because they are, according to their inkling, inside
 someone else,
they already came out of him ... Then they reek,
and, because apart from all that, there is usually sultry
 heat,
they begin to decompose ... What else is left to them
 afterwards
but to approach God with God?
But that's exactly it: we observe the Sun's eclipse
exactly only through a tinted glass ...

AT THE NIGHT OF AMAZEMENT

He stood at the shore with a burning tree in his hand
and held the light for the one who was swimming across
    the river,
clinging to the bushy tail of a horse ...
When she came to him, he didn't say:
"There, where I come from, the whole forest is aflame."
And when he embraced her, she didn't say: "There, where I
    come from,
a woman from Samara is still at the well ..."

Both kept silent ... At first,
because they were lived by what can't be expressed,
and later because they lived the word for its image only ...

A SUNDAY AFTERNOON AT A PRAGUE SUBURB

Sultry heat, walloped with a golden bag, is splitting
this stinking suburb with dizziness,
as far as the consciousness of the street,
where, today at last, someone appears,
who, a long time ago, walked out from burnt Ilium.
How firm he is in his youth!
And yet, despite all his self-confident silence,
with seven lips on seven leaves of kissing,
and despite all his self-confident radiance, knowledgeable
of the crosscut through a brick wall, and concentrated
upon an obstinate entrance –
he looks like an approximate one ...
This may be because he is wearing a ready-made suit,
or because he is not ruthless enough to recognize
that he is reaching his goal.
But yes! he already enters,
and will soon see that, in an abattoir,
they still use dross for bedding mute creatures ...

AN EXPECTATION

You waited for moonrise and there came a prostitute.
Wanting to light a kerosene lamp, she said:
"Today at hairdresser's, there was an old lady.
Oh, what a wish list she had! She was never
satisfied, everything was not coppery enough!
When, about one hour later, she was supposed to stand up,
it turned out that she was dead.
Isn't it a beautiful death? Better, indeed,
than to hang oneself on one's own plait!"
"Yes," I answered her, "but don't light the lamp!"
And as if you wanted to put her forward
by the unexpected eclipse of the moon
into something that may come one year later,
you said: "There is some cocaine under the mattress, if
 you'd like! ...
In the meantime, I'll wait for the sunrise."

WOMAN AND WORD

Man sings or lies ... A single pearl button
on the whole dress of his beloved is enough for him,
a single defect on her naked beauty ...
But when the gilded heaviness of dishevelled passion
retracts his goatlike eye into the close-fisted outlines of
    emptiness,
which would prefer not to be witnessed,
he remains cowardly silent ... Silent to the denial
of a silent soul ... Or is he, perhaps, losing his voice only
    because
he, with foreboding, relies on one single working word,
which again only a woman can pronounce?

A CHILD

A child, with its ear on the rail,
is listening to a train ...
Being lost in omnipresent music,
it truly cares little
whether the train is approaching or running away ...
It's only you who always waited for someone,
always took leave of someone,
until you found yourself and are nowhere more ...

EN ROUTE

In the tavern near a lake, they offered you a swan for
> dinner.
You refused and, with some bad rum in your pocket,
you climbed a nearby hill.
Countless swarms of hens and geese
were all that you could see in the village below.
This made you understand all at once that the bad people
> from the tavern
knew the evil one well and wanted to revere him ...

AT A RURAL GRAVEYARD DURING THE VILLAGE WAKE

Here, where fresh reeking of starlings
makes the air lighter, yes, here,
where even female thighs would become wings,
here, yes, exactly here are we the blindest,
and a digger's shovel would have to be illuminated
perhaps by only one single moon, yet by all the suns,
so that we would understand that love's intimacies
come from a threat ...
But, down there in the village, they planted the tree
    of dance
and now trample the earth around it
so it can sprout more ...

MINKOWSKI'S WORLD

There are matters resulting from dismay. They turn pale
  like informers,
avoid movement, names, even sex,
and concentrate themselves on the last moment
before the creation of the world ... Which does not mean
that we know the time when they started to be ...
Well then, in a crushing black ice of desire,
in order, at least, to be and to be in the present,
we gratefully give ear to an oriole's song,
which calls: "Buy some glue!" –
and, like witnesses, we give ear to the roar of the village
  bull,
in whom they are implanting, in front of the almshouse,
  an artificial eye.

THE END?

What a time: impertinent in the extreme,
cocky and threatening, as it used to be
when the last pagan god died ...

And what an eternity: hopeful, beseeched,
like the last hour before the coming of Jesus Christ.
But it forbids itself everything ...

EVA II

Evermore she moves from a virgin into a virgin, she, always
    to be filled up,
and hence towards the future.
And it is, therefore, a precious, ageless moment
if she stops in the present and looks back at you.
Thereafter her glance
is as amorous as it is inquiring,
and you are allowed to answer it with your own destruction.
Yet if you are free of melancholy,
you have already committed an offence against her beauty ...

AT A WEDDING

Only one bird-cherry, left at one time for seeds,
was cutting all bleating windows
with the glazier's diamond of scent
to let out the music that likes talking about space,
but at the same time looks around full of fright like someone
who urinates in a forbidden place.
A tottery raving of banqueters,
crackled in the eyes like the enamel of some china,
was tearing up the sustained musical notes
into a protruding or saucy timidity,
which was looking for a rescue in everything that had the
    name of shrubs.
Then everything was returning into the house place again ...
But a drunken bride,
who had on as many frocks as a frog has cloaks,
was so beautiful that no one could see her,
and she then easily pressed under her knee
the finger of her first lover ...

THE EARTH

From the outside so bare that those who are alive belittle her,
in its inside so pellucid that all the dead can see us.

From the outside so motherly that it buries those who live,
in its inside so naked that it wakes up the dead.

From the outside so fully in the soul that those who live are only corpses,
in its inside so full of bones that the dead are immortal.

From the outside so modest that it resides over everything,
in its inside so victorious that it has renounced all!

WITHOUT A FUNERAL

In the woods so deep that you had to think
about hidden reasons and about the negation
    of coincidences,
you spotted, close to a lazing moss,
a handful of ribs, washed clean like a curd press,
a nose, a wig and a tin button.
Without trying to prove that the dead man was left-handed,
there, next to some scattered nails, the last strawberry
    of the Indian summer
lived and was so ruddy that your fear was burning,
your nakedness insecure
and your consciousness irritable ...
Down in the village you were later told: He was returning
from our village fair. The night was dark,
by a pretty penny less. He might have lost his way.
And what didn't fit into the boar's stomach
was taken apart by ants and foxes ...

TWO LIVES

When, for some time, we were standing on the village
	green
and observing the romping wind in the skirt of straw,
Lao-tse said: The life inside a book
can never be what feeds itself by music.
Though the desire of both is heavenly,
in vain are they linked together at the weddings of gods ...
One of them knows that the present time is not merely
	today's day,
the other knows that it is indeed a secret which can't be
	concealed,
and both of them know that secret has to appear by itself.
This humility brings them inadvertently near each other
in their lives of pure and simple mortals ...

LOVERS III

They meet secretly behind the bier shed,
where dusk is giving them a name,
and the nettle a bare foot.
Yet because even here they would have to serve a sentence
for whatever certainty (with an eye on a future murder in
 their family),
they soon disappear towards the only vinegar green on the
 constricting horizon,
but they have already disappeared there along their own
 way,
contemptuously, even reproachfully, and in such a way
as though Eve's primeval search,
of Eve before the apple was plucked off,
was tempting them back to the tree ...

A COUNTRYSIDE

These two hillocks, like knees
pressed into the trousers of the verdure,
do not deny a viper in the crotch of granite.
A little lower, a pond shivers,
a diaphragm cut out of Swift's belly.
And lower still, but already bodiless,
some dung tries with oppressive heat to fill up
the head of a mythical tossing about ...
And only the sky is hot-headed, headstrong,
and crooked with the wrongs done to you,
and it shares, consciously, everything that you are still not
and that you are, in order to be at all ...

INSIDE OUT

It might have been a single movement of a funnel man,
overfilling a glass with wine,
that caused some rivers to never see the ocean
because they disappear in the desert.

And it might have been a single stamp of a cow,
squelching colchicum,
that caused us not to know what innocence was,
because cognition gladly steps aside
when facing the essence of murderers ...

PATIENT DUSK

What was impossible for the violent hyperboles of the
    spirit,
popping up from the interval when wine meets wine,
sheer dust, into which the recognized platitude urinated,
is now mirrored in the likeness of heavens full of crows,
and in the Perseid's fall, itchingly untouchable
like scabies on Buddha's belly button ...

A WINTER NIGHT

Frost, clean shaven. Frost, spreading around rolled plate
    glass,
behind which a man of the lake is turning pages of a book
under a grassweed of the lamp. He is enthused and turns
    pale
and disputes all that's not a little bell at the hermitage,
as if only a night without women could be a poem's
    measure,
which is subconsciously despised by no one ...

SLEEPLESSNESS

At its sleeplessness (which hinders you from imagining
whether a larch is without needles in winter),
today's night has strangled and squeezed now for too long ...
Does it really have so much sooty and shagged linen
that the last withdrawing cloud
will catch the dawn at a rinsing place only as an old woman
who needs a compliment: "God grant you all as white!"?

AT THE END OF AUGUST

The horse, who yesterday carried a bride
and today is working at a whim gin,
might be, by its outermost turning around a bridegroom's
    courting,
repeating the revolving circle of the wedding night,
the circle around a reluctant centre,
but a centre which liberates the seed ...

Yet what to do with the wheat, if the bride is proud?
Oh, don't be afraid, as early as one month later,
she will walk across the village green
in a lady's shoes made of altar-bread dough ...

LEGACY

What poets leave behind
always has its innermost harmed by time, sins, exile.
The most genuine one of them,
the most unknown one, the most silent and most loving
    one
would not for the world force himself upon you: neither by
    a parable,
nor by contempt, nor by solace, less so by love...
Being present, he is already absent ... And Picasso,
making a snowman, comprehended correctly
that the immortality of art
is in time, in sins, in exile,
which have to be redeemed by the sun
into tears, a fountain, a river, a sea, into nothing ...

OCTOBER

The air is so pellucid that it rules out
any likeness ... Even a double
refuses to give phantasmal evidence that we are alive ...
Invisibility rises to such a fury
that we simply close our eyes ...
A good wine is alone in itself ... Art, too.

FROM THE DARKNESS

When the hand of a virgin was covering his shame,
feathery, uncertain like wonder coming incognito,
he remembered that we were made of the soil of the earth.

Only the dead are already so countless
that earth may still be earth,
but soil is no soil any more ...

IN HELL AS WELL

Why a cat sucking at Picasso's brush
could not remind us of women's desire,
mentally inhibited so much
that one of them (in particular when hearing a saddle
 squeaking)
opens the horse's artery and drinks blood,
and another overgrows her face with a nun's beard?

The simplicity of danger extorted
the present, which, so far, is always scant.
And God, almost human, is in hell as well ...

BEFORE A FIG

A red string of the prostitute Rahab
was forcing the mute self-abnegation of a man to an all-
 night talk,
while the woman, in her thoughts, carted the wood
for burning phalli to death ... But the man was also
 drinking
and thus quenching the burning stakes, quenching them
 with the sentiment
that can seldom live to see, because everybody becomes
 frightened,
while the woman, her skirt burnt through on her belly,
and hearing a downpour outside
and thinking about the spell of torpidity the saints feel,
said bitterly and, in fact, from her groin:
"Evil inside you is alive not because you breathe,
but because you are innocent!"

IDOLS FROM THE CYCLADES

A moon ray, falling upon the idols from the Cyclades,
reflects itself from vaginal lips to a laurel wand of a genius.
It would be already too much,
if we, in a truncated game for everything,
admitted that it is the word that acts,
but that it is the spirit that creates.
Yet, with our loins, we worship
passion instead of languor in a man,
and predisposition instead of longing in a woman ...

ON THE FIRST SUNDAY IN LENT

O bitterness, bitterness, you, so much of this world
and yet you, who are returning from the other world
exactly at the moment when a postman comes
with secretly opened letters!

O poesy, poesy, you, so much from the other world,
and yet you who does not have to return
because there are voices of birds, extinct long ago,
who are still alive in the music of barbarian dances.

O you, the bitterness of poesy, you, so much of this world
because from the other world,
you who know well that poets are giving the word
that they would like to take back later.
God, however, is always in the future ...

ANYWHERE I

On a rainy night, in which there is no place
for any intervention of yours –
or in frost, which lets people perish,
in a hungry frost, which might be God
if God exists in the loss of senses –
in all our lives, in which there is no touching
because we are only the closeness of two contra-radiations,
the blackmailing hope says to an assassin, who is still in
    the egg:
"If you won't be born, I'll give birth to myself!" ...

ANYTIME IN SEPTEMBER

The trees start withering like a tanner's skin,
and the air grows heavy with what they lose in their weight.
A falling leaf, the auger of a baroque column,
drills a faucet into the stone for leave-taking tears of
    nightingales,
who will soon refuse to drink water from the drowned;
everything is seven times the place that is sagging
due to the tabes dorsalis of space;
the lightest egg has its embryo as far as limbo –
and only man is offered the steps to the gallows
or a Daedalean crosscut through a cloud ...

DALILA

Even evil is from God ... But as a deity is more than God;
malice, the total malice of a woman, blamed for a winter
     light
and tainted with the screaming soot of a ventral rupture,
will multiply the devil by acquitting itself of both its
     numbness and its word
and by standing astride for awhile in the door of a mill or a
     still house,
her hips propped up,
her belly sprinkled with cinders of superfine black flour
and her rectum prolapsed.
Her look is useful in the basket for artificial eyes,
her complexion is speckled like the floor after a decorator
     has left,
and her breath is so sharp
that the air becomes dry goods ...
But the woman in childbed made her mind up long ago.
She decided to bury her child in a dung yard
and Samson's cut-off entitlements in an ant-hill ...

JUST TO STEP IN

A room, not heated for a long time,
so much without shape that, at one blow of orphanhood,
there appears a hollow likeness –
and that, when you have entered, you hear the cracking roar of all
who, during the burning of knee tendons,
prefer silence to repentance!

A room, not heated for a long time, in which you understand
that those who live deny to those alive the word of the soul blinded by the body,
those who are dying to the dying ones the word of the body blinded by the soul,
and those who are dead to the dead the vision
of themselves!

MELAMPYGOS

Even to the highest ones, both to Apollo, with the curved
    snake of his lyre,
and to Martius, with the stretching root of his flute,
it used to be a relief to enter a harlot house,
coated with ruddle and gypsum,
those truly common paints, which however, clinging and
    sagging,
indicated the bulgy service of women
and leeches lodged into a vein.
But it used to happen even to the highest ones
that they launched out in saddles into the ascetic nature,
and if it were not for Herakles, the black-ass,
who ran under the legs of their horses,
no temples with columns only in the front
would have arisen,
and the destruction of whole cities
would never have come ...

FROM THE HISTORY I

Serpent, as constellation, was far too intimate to women
to be contemptuous of their wedding night,
in which they copulated with a god,
muddy up to the ears of celery.

Men, on the other hand, preferred the most distant
    goddesses.
They slept with them and congested them with images,
and, till today, they admire a toilet duct
that survived the palace of Knoss.

A HEREDITARY ONE

When the pips of Eve's apple
permeated man's ventral haughtiness
and fell then into the grass of a once tenacious paradise,
the earth closed round like a refusing woman.
If, soon after, the rain had not stuck out its scowling finger
from the shoulders of a cloud and had not pointed to the
    moment's water,
in which nature, like a woman, washes everything
that, narrowed down to a line during the day
and to a precipice during the night,
resembles a cat's eye –
the trees, barren at that time, might not have
needed to testify to all of dying,
but only to a part of death ...

THREE

A sculptor and a tanner! Maybe only these two,
in the time that is killing itself like a cockatrice
by looking in the mirror,
are discerning the whole of eternity, bestowed to be
    devoured
by the eye-tail of Venus's vulva –
or the belly fat of Lot's wife, pickled
in the salt mines of animals ...
In the meantime, a poet gives testimony to feasts and songs
in the house of kvass, in the house of funerals;
his desire for an ascending revival
grasps for the wine that gives a testimonial
only as a certificate of poverty,
while the heart-valve prolapse of poesy
struggles agonizingly for the full pulse of a *joyful* God ...

A SOUND AND A FOOTSTEP

A sound, some sort of a gentle sound,
nurtured by the fat from an Apollo's leg.
Yet a footstep, some sort of a toilsome footstep,
drinking the sweat of a mortal.
The sound on the way to a fortune-teller;
The footstep on the way to a double!

Truly, indeed:
whose the simile is, his too is time in Art ...

PARAKLIT

A night, guessing from a sound at a prison yard,
time, guessing from a tone at the forgetting of words,
irons, guessing from a name at the first sin
with a question when and what kind the last one will be ...
And with all that, you alone,
alone with the uniqueness of inspiration, summarized into
    bliss,
but a bliss which is disintegrating
into innumerable fears of itself ...

MEZZA DI VOCE

But there is music, the woman of all masculine ...
How often, in the world of simple human beauty,
it had no spare time for the created creating,
which is giving it a thoroughbred name,
known intimately only to some gods,
but to all murderers, to whom a fallen angel brought
    pleasure,
and who didn't share it with him in a devilish manner ...

TEMPTATION

The storm brought nothing but another swelter,
as greasy as the smell of a scalded hen.
The wretched squinting of little dead-end lanes
cuts holes into the ice of melted women.
The fee at a public toilet
rings on the clouds of the lost sense of smell.
The great Purple Emperor of time would want to give credit
to one more definite sign at least,
but today even the children's talk can hardly be persuasive,
and your heart too is uncertain,
closed in the hollowed absence of illusions
only with half eyes, which, after they added death,
are slipping the stitch of life's end ...

AS IN A DREAM

At every place where his pilgrim staff touched the earth,
the voice of some of the dead resounded,
of those who died a long time ago, according to the
    appearance of time,
of those who have died just now, according to the truth of
    the Infinite.
He lent his ear to all of them ... And as if the voices
of those who used to have wings here were the last ones,
and as if the first ones were the voices of gravediggers.
But all that just appeared so.
Well, even he hasn't started yet at all ...

ICE IS CRACKING

A banquet finished a long time ago, and a visitor is coming
  only now.
Not knowing what to do with your fright,
which is hardly helped by the roar
of cracking ice behind the windows;
he would love to imagine himself with a more definite
  appearance.
But while he gives way to the spirits,
he goes relentlessly to encounter you –
and you, suddenly and somehow entrusted, start to
  understand
that you must not love in order to be loved,
that you must not love and be loved,
that you must not love because you love,
but that you must love the one who doesn't love you ...

A STORM IN THE MOUNTAINS

Why did a house come into existence? Maybe actually
just for lighting up a watch candle there during a storm ...
And we do the same and enjoy doing it
because life is truly light,
and then even the Devil seems to be in God.
Under a tottery parable, a girl brings wine,
and her appearance reminds us, through our naked eye,
that we are still alive,
and that the mortality of beauty is still shining ...
but not until it runs out of its shine will it become a star.

A SWAN

A quondam slap that Lucretia gave to her defiler
dies away in the swan, not frightened until today
and buffeting the genial water with her wing ...
Ostensibly, gigantic space between both acts
shivers from hatred to heaviness all the way to history,
to the history which is too often aflame,
to the history in which a boy fears for his stuffed bird,
and in which a little girl is afraid
that her doll may die in a fire ...
Hatred towards heaviness? But when the king Sargon
jumped off his horse and went on foot,
his soldiers lifted and carried his horse.

PELASGIANS

Pelasgians were not concerned about the chatter of
 boulders,
piled up into the air, piled up hot-headedly
because they were piled up exactly at the time
when the black wildlife was fattest.
But how beautiful it is that they didn't stack them
for covering their nakedness ... On the contrary,
they used to leave cracks there,
and during the gauntness of the spring, being one-eyed,
with a pockmarked smile, they watched through those
 cracks
a comforted child, swinging while holding firm on the ring
hinged in the nostrils of a bull ...

A PREMONITION

On a December night, you filled up the glass of your hard
 drinking with wine
and went away into the adjacent room for a book ...
When, after a while, you returned, the glass was half
 empty.
Swallowing your fear through the glottis of insanity,
you asked who had taken a sip from it, since you were living
 alone,
erratically surrounded with the thorny stone of walls,
and you asked about this with such a barbarity
that you repelled, long ago, both the statue, and the
 monster, and the ghost ...

A NOTE

This is the way we live through it:
a tree, barely in bloom, loses its leaves
in permanent bloom and permanent losing.
And our fiery laziness and impatience
are so persistent that they authentically
compete with eternity.
We cannot be otherwise, for indeed:
if God's joy is our strength,
how do we not weaken when God grieves ...

A PRISON AND A SHEEPFOLD

A hairy scratch into the plaster or a cut into a tree will do
to become Eve's furnace ...
A furnace, a cold furnace, but still a furnace
in front of which a prisoner or a forsaken shepherd
burns all their images by the finger alphabet
of the deaf and dumb ... A protruding motion
and passion, tapping at some imaginary adversity,
can, at the end, do nothing else but return into themselves,
weakened, sooty and with a revengeful swearword ...

MOTHER

Have you ever seen your old mother
at the moment when she is making your bed for you,
tucking in, stretching, smoothing and caressing the
 bedsheet,
lest a single pinching crease be there?
Her breath, the motion of her hand and her palm
are so caring
that, gone by, they quench the fire in Persepolis,
and, present, they have already calmed a certain future
 storm
on a Chinese or some other, not-yet-known sea ...

A STILL LIFE AT A LAKE

Yes, everything is here! And everything here is so perfect,
everything at its place; silence is here, loftiness, even
    radiance;
wisdom is here, dusted off in a manly way, bread and even
    books;
no, no hair will get onto your pen here,
so you don't have to wipe it with your sleeve;
here you know well that a wine cellar bears only wine,
elements of nature are here too, wind, stars, a storm –
and yet you are fabricating names for sails,
in a desire to run away ...

Once you have dreamt them out, yes, maybe even earlier,
your escape becomes as real as that monk long ago
who left the god-home Olympus only because
he couldn't find any goddesses there ...

A VOICE

At dusk, as venomous as January
around the house which one heats with lignite coke,
in the street where some snot,
still flicked out freely by a boy,
gives evidence about the road to a reformatory
at dusk,
where snow is suspected of a barbers' napkin
fallen out from a ragman's dosser of thaw,
between walls, built up by a drunkard's grief
from red blots on the face of dead poets,
you suddenly heard the following:
However black may be the soul, it can hardly persuade the body
about the needlessness of life, unless a self-murderer doesn't believe in soul.
And then, in order to deserve this disbelief,
the soul would have to kill itself earlier than the body would do ...
And it can't do that because it didn't give itself life.

FROM A VILLAGE

I remember well: it was a beautiful summer day
around noon ... Dung beetles were working in a cowpat,
while a lizard ran over my book
and, out of embarrassment, cleared its throat in raspberry
   canes.
Then dogs began to bark, an indication
that the postman had arrived.
Being summoned to the gate of the gamekeeper's lodge,
I met there "the local crackbrain,"
called in at the same time ...
Truly sinister news arrived for me then,
and for him – his precious dole.
Such a tangy moment was impossible for him to support,
even if he knew that cymbals hefted only nine kilograms;
such a moment was giving him hope
for all the cheese in the world and a candyfloss:
such a moment was for him so mind blowing
and so ceremonious that, when he was to countersign
a receipt for that trifle,
he began to shudder and asked almost wildly,
"Do I have to pull off my coat?"

CLAY

When man chews away by himself and hears his chewing,
it's with a spinal fright that he suddenly begins to
    comprehend clay;
not some backfill but the kind
that was scattered around with a palm.
Lowermost, like an already buried body,
it despises the results of battles;
at the highest point, like a speech, and the speech like
    a soul's face,
it has a strong desire for some gin for the graveyard
    caretaker ...

HOR

Hor, chopping off the testes of Sutech,
he indeed emasculated evil. Sutech, however,
(even without poets) had his double ...
If everything here is a parable,
then his chimera, rotten till death,
and yet godlike as God is and thus immortal,
is today (thanks to poets)
nearer to us than the fleeting reality.

VERSES

She said to you: No one out of those
who are not killed until the autumn,
who didn't come even in the summer ...
He said to you: Yes, but the troops of Xerxes move through
    the winter already,
and those who are following them
(women, eunuchs, beasts of burden and dogs)
will not be slaughtered before the spring ...
The summer may be suitable
just for dusty crushing of dead men's bones
in scenery where only the straight flight of a bird shows
that the river is sloping down there ...

WITH A KNIFE INTO THE HEART

Who would like to tell lies here, again and again,
and put on an appearance as if love couldn't leave bruises?
From the little ear of a girl, which they will pierce for an
 earring,
there is only a little step to a forcible lifting of a golden
 chemise –
and both Lucretia and Dante
(both of them insincere in their sensuality,
and quarrelsome from the virtue that degrades)
then look in vain for an ideal murderer ...
In vain! For even a simple local murderer,
who, after having completed his commitment, moistens his
 finger
in the spilled blood in order to assure himself
that the blood really is warm;
as a perpetual Cain's brother,
he hopes also in his fate: that no one finds him,
and no one kills him ...

LOVERS IV

They walk through a forest ... And albeit through a deep
 forest,
in vain he wheedles her, lies to her, and changes his voice.
She is afraid that someone could see them ...
In vain he tells her that men fall to their knees
in order to pray; that they kneel in order to make love;
that it's our new generation we take on our knees.
She is afraid that someone could see them ...
In vain he whispers to her: Imagine that in five years
we will have been together for five years then,
and we won't regret it.
She is afraid that someone could see them ...
In vain then he keeps silent, and symbolically he is
 drowning
at the height of her womb, swallowing the water of his lust.
She is afraid that someone could see them ...
And not until they both, unwillingly, frightened away
 a deer,
her sensual shyness, reassured by the shyness that is not
 human,
turns into such a passion that it tears her skirt, her chemise
 and her body ...

AN ANCIENT WOMAN

"In the ears of peonies, the cancer of my womb is
 humming,"
said the forlorn T ... "And the white creaking half-tone,
heard once, long time ago, when a cue was chalked,
only emphasizes, with the diffused stench of a cheesy skin,
that there is nothing that could help me ...
They were tossing me up then from the bed sheet of my
 youth and beauty
into the hollow height of their lusts ...
They were breathing it in, they were changing their voices,
and their hind legs were invisible ...
You can't imagine the weight
of a human skin when freshly flayed ...
Having known nothing about the spring with the lewd
 whims
of pregnant women, I didn't quite care
about the trickle of a female washbowl,
and, after four pockets spilled out and the fifth one empty,
I opened my heart to a dream ... And the result was a child,
weaned by a bottle in and out of pubs,
and then an impudently wide and vast emptiness
between the shoulder blades and the heart,
an emptiness, shortened by steps into a pawn shop,
and now one vomit of the excrement through fate's throat,
an excrement that I couldn't wipe up even with the paper
manufactured from the bark of the Tree of Knowledge ..."

AN ODE

O life – yes, you! Still only you!
You, in a friendly conversation and a kindly shaken hand,
you, in the deeds of good will because of heart's hope,
you, nameless in the gifts, as the dead give
and the living accept and entrust further again,
you, free, because of the very motion of love,
you, always you. O Life,
even if the bell-shaped measure of an evening ear
can suddenly ignite evil from evil,
you, ever silent like a crime,
and peaceful like funeral music
so the horses won't be startled –
and yet, you again in a modestly shaken hand
and a friendly conversation –
O Life, yes, you, in which I don't tell lies
if I truly say that I love ...
yet, O Life, in which I feel with the same truthfulness,
that a self-murderer is too candid
to become a poet ...

JUNE

Sultriness, swollen sky-high by the hyperbole of a pig's
    bladder ...
Everything puffs up or cringes down ...
A scientist, having blinded a sexton beetle,
observes it and is surprised
that, after all, it found its carcass,
and that its eyes are somehow extra ...
Though badly exserted, human veins
still can't smear, with all their pulses,
the raptures in the old furniture of the Sun ...
The tree of butterflies is ailing from the white grubs of
    aeroplanes ...
And only a gardener, paralysed during watering,
lies close to the hose, as if he let his member grow
from the dust as far as the peonies ...

NIGHT AFTER NIGHT

Only a virgin can enter her own chamber
through a closed door,
where everything with the name of an assurance
has already long been scented with a tapestry of self-abuse,
violence, spitting into the well or a pitch-black wreath
thrown, of its own accord, upon the man's tower.
If he is a poet, everything will be spoiled,
if he is an assassin, then nakedness will be here,
and an applauder will be here, the applauder,
hired from the marble quarries of Aeschylus ...

A TESTIMONY

More than once every month the sun changes,
and more than once every year it intrudes with all its rays
into an old temple
and gaily illuminates the statues of kings,
who lie on the tombstones
and clasp with their stingy hands a little bag,
filled up with their hearts and entrails.

More than once every month a star changes,
and many times every year it intrudes
with some of its rays into a morgue
and, with a splattering laugh of a choking being,
forces the neighbouring bicyclists to ride across celery.

Four times every month the moon changes,
but only once a year it intrudes into the little shop
of a shopkeeper who sells old hats.
Only once a year, and only with one ray.
It is seized so much by terror!

THE ROPE LADDER

The rope ladder of Romeo!
How easily it flounces in a vesper wind,
so fine that it holds back even its hempen soul!
He who descended it understands the greatness of man,
which, if it were not dishonoured here, would be
    incomplete ...
And he who is ascending it
lives a passion, full-blooded and young enough,
so as to be able to wait for an echo,
but a passion too godlike
lest it destroy itself by its own fire ...

FROM HISTORY II

The rain which destroyed grapes
takes its revenge on the waiting desert by leaving it out.
The desert thus learned that its knowledge prevents its
 existence,
the desert so white that it suspects everything of stains,
the desert so clean that it is inhuman,
the desert so cruel because it does not sin,
the desert that will take its revenge ...

You think about those paper mitres
of heretics burnt to death ...

YES OR NO?

Forever are we looking for the centre ... But, being a point,
it is blind ... Looking for our hearts,
we are looking for blindness ... And having been blind for
    a long time now,
we are just touching.
The touch that assures itself with all its excuses
that there will always be the rich and the poor,
not because the body is full or hungry,
but because every human soul is different ...
And, in fact, it's a mere sense of touch
that fumbles infallibly about
in the diverging lanes of a slave market ...

LIFE II

Hamlet told me: "You know it: suddenly nothing, absolutely nothing,
absolutely nothing more is facing us, nothing like the moment
when even the future seems to be behind us.
He who loves should rejoice!

Except that the universe though allegedly completed is also unlimited.
Man suddenly feels lonely, woman shivers with cold;
ergo, they haven't killed themselves. They come together
and are grateful that once more they can see something of their fate
even if it is a shamelessly precise
journey into a poorhouse ..."

STAY WITH ME

Stay with me awhile, don't leave me alone,
there is so much emptiness in my fate
that it's only you who prevents my proud humility
from questioning nothing more!

Stay with me awhile, don't leave me alone,
have mercy on my impatience,
which, lazily recorded in the logbook of a prison ship,
is so permanent that it almost rivals eternity!

Stay with me awhile, don't leave me alone,
you are not good at being angry, you don't keep being
    angry –
and where would you go and where would you be
when you get over it? ... Wait for a while, wait,
wait at least until that time
when the postman comes with letters just for you!

ANYWHERE II

The evening is so beautiful that you are bashful to even
　　　desire
from the depth of your lonely emptiness ...
The dead, as if walking over each other in the worms of
　　　a graveyard,
a beast, as if being frightened by a butcher's apron,
things, as if not knowing where they are ...
Yes, it is written that no one will behold God when alive.
He spares us then, when he suffers a faint,
lives in the fire, in the fog, in the cloud, in the wind,
and walks in theatre curtains and in the future ...

Even the saints caught a glimpse only of his back.

MOSES

Who spoke with God and then wanted to speak later with
    people
must have had horns ...
For until now, we have not always believed
until a miracle or a tragedy had happened,
and even then only as few,
so few of us that even twins have fallen out
arguing that both had grey hair,
but that only one of them was grey just in the front ...

CLARITY

An evening and a lamp ... And that moment
when an aging poet has nothing more to question,
tired of the bovine face of both mirages and real things,
and overburdened by the spirit-comforter ...

The last *visible* one among us
was Jesus Christ.

SPIRITUAL RETREAT

Two trees were in Paradise ...
It's true that by eating from the Tree of Knowledge
we indeed became mortal
but also similar to gods ...

From Paradise, though, we were expelled,
so that already knowing good and evil
we should also taste
from the Tree of Life,
because then, we would become immortal
even as men ...

IT DOES NOT HAVE TO BE, BUT

It does not have to be a large hill of the night
to let anybody feel
that we are still playing on the bestial boards
left over from Noah's ark.

It does not have to be a large hill of the dawn
to let anybody see from it
that it is still the same tram which carries people
to work, to a graveyard, or to a hospital.

But it might always be the very hollow of the day,
in which someone is going to suffer
from the impatience of the one who is a messenger,
and, at the same time, who is listening to the message ...

WHEN LISTENING TO A GRAMOPHONE RECORD

Only today they pluck a pheasant somewhere,
which was supposed to be served at the table of Sargon the
    king.
Only today a double quartertone of birds, long extinct,
is alive in the music of savage dances.
Only today an ordinary diphtheria of cave graffiti
is finding its animal glory in the throat of an opera.
Only today tantalite and bezoar
are to be seen in the underbelly of a statue, begun long
    ago.

Nothing returns from the other world. Everything is here.
But even the one of us who is already inside
has to be still on his way in ...

THE STAR FOR ONE SECOND ONLY

Snow is falling ... And its most silent landing
puts the very last black on the roar of coal, unloaded
    somewhere.
Furthermore, two weddings at the same time
trample the street with a sweetheart's script.
Some white meat, some black varnish ... An action, not
    a hustle.
Then it turns dark ... But even the best from the possible
    ones
don't understand and consider a concealed, selfish
    irritation,
momentary and dumb, as joy,
while suffering is what will voice all that later –
this star for one second only, radiating and confirming
    eternity ...

ALWAYS AHEAD OF

Second-rate wine, drunk from the casks of famous whores'
 breasts,
can hardly contain a finer baseness than this night's
 downpour.
Instead of beating into stones,
bespattered with blood like a staircase to a dentist,
the rain promises a hymen even in the ear of a graveyard,
or inflammation in the eye of adultery ...

No thought of repentance.
Our hairdo falls asleep
always ahead of our hair ...

FOR EVERYONE

Wandering along a few corridors leading to an apartment
and returning from few apartments leading to the corridor –
you have grasped that whose today's hope is
will also have a heresy ...
We may be waiting
until empty purgatory is completely empty.
Though hell is so overcrowded
that it still has enough room for all of us ...

A SAINT

He, the hard one, and hard maybe only because
there was no rock nearby,
He, present through the nature he didn't care about,
and expected by the city, where the ugliness of his face
was called beauty
because his face would mirror itself in an excited freedom
which they would try in vain to slow down ...
But he, he in himself without himself,
he who was living a life of a saint longer than he was
    supposed to,
the life of a saint that was already becoming a habit ...

At the moment when it seemed that a little more of joy
and he would have died, nomads arrived.
They broke his teeth and had a fight
for the golden bridge he spat out.
Then they shaved his private parts,
attached some leeches to his anus,
twisted off his testicles, sewed up his eyes with tinsel,
and sent him out against the sun ...

AN ATOM

In the motion of nature, there is something so new today
that you say to yourself: yes, at one time, Heaven was first,
and Earth was first, but they perished,
perished together with a copulating prophet ...

In the motion of nature, there is something so new today
that you ask yourself, full of terror: is compassion love?
Or are we, in truth, already in the branches?
And after we have reached the fruit,
do we have to be bodiless?

AN EPOCH

We have never been the whole. We have only resembled,
but resembled to the full.
Now, when we begin to become an aggregate,
we try ourselves only as a portion of our likeness,
which, in the future, we shall totally leave.
What may become of us?...

ALONG THE WAY

Every bridge is somehow buying us off.
This one, we all crossed so far
despite being overloaded with mortal sins.
And yet, under a girl, kissed by a man for the first time,
it will shortly break down ...

Yes, I understand that it is not the lot of mystery
to have to persuade us,
when it is already too much to be tested at all.
But in such a cruel way? In such a cruel way?
Oh, have pity on us, God,
in your distrust, in your jealousy!

SHE II

Beauty is from God. But beauty tempts.
From the man in Paradise to the coroner
examining a murdered prostitute;
it accuses us of our loneliness,
it betroths us to a woman like some future,
but the future in such a way
as if it believed in an eternity behind God.
Then it tolerates us through our fear –
and if we are jealous, it smiles lecherously
as far as where languor changes us into joy from evil ...

Compared with poverty as a certainty,
beauty is too wavering as to injure the majority ...
Perceived, yes – seen, not!

A CONFESSION

How am I supposed to be grateful to you
that you are so close and that I have a place to go to
when desire sweats through the Universe so inhumanely
till poverty as a certainty returns it into time?
To have somewhere to go, even if you are one of those
    women
who despise an ardent word only for the reason
that it was uttered in drunkenness!

How am I supposed to be grateful to you
that you are so slow, when my evil
is faster than inspiration?
Only for a moment I forgot about you,
and the night grew so much stronger
that it opened by itself the door to my flat,
from where your absence
moved me out in a hurry ...

ALREADY NOW

Even heaven will come to an end ... From a Chaldean priest
to the magic of Thessaly and the kidneys of Aztecs,
all is but debris ... After they've added a hint,
they narrow the sign ... Who is talking about completeness?

But even a female stigma in front of the taproom of the
    spring,
even the roar of flies on St. Wenceslas Day
falling into the plum jam
are not complete, though they might have sputtered,
underbellies closer towards adultery ...

Even evil we learn to know only partly.
It is the lot of saints, the allotment of mortals
and of the rest – it is just the difference ...

YES

An autumnal evening, drooping in the admiration
    of lovers.
And, at an ageing poet's, a windowpane,
mushroomed by a stone into a daddy longlegs spider,
and a measles-like sumptuousness of candles,
which, close to midnight, will be replaced by a kerosene
    lamp,
borrowed from the cowshed ...

So far, he always managed with a little bit of something:
a heart's twitch, as if by a rapier of an illegal shape,
the heels of rain, treading Our Lady's tears,
a sunray, disguised as some blind dots
on the belly of a woman's dress, an intermezzo of curiosity –
so that, being cumbersome to ceremonious memories,
he found himself straight back in his childhood ...

Even today, having caught sight of a migratory speck
    of soot,
even today it is in him, and yet he feels
that until now he never gave a kiss to an empty bottle
unless he had another one full in front of him.
And somehow belittled and then daring
and too impatient in his hour
so that to be regretful in his time,
he draws near to God as a child with no rights

who urges on God with God,
because as a man, who knows the screw-thread of a snake,
he should have knelt down earlier ...

ON THE ADVANCE

Nothing can excuse a poet, not even his death.
And yet, from his hazardous existence,
a few signs always remain
somewhat in excess. And in these,
certainly not any perfection, even if it were Paradise,
but truthfulness, even if it should be Hell ...

Translation: Josef Tomáš
Foreword: Jiří Brabec
Illustrations and graphic design: Jáchym Šerých
Typography: Veronika Plátková

Published 2011 by arima publishing

Lightning Source UK, Ltd.
Milton Keynes UK

www.ingramcontent.com/pod-product-compliance
Lightning Source LLC
Chambersburg PA
CBHW071302110426
42743CB00042B/1142